a servant's dance: give your life 生 away

çì-ẏàì

a servant's dance: give your life 生 away

Copyright © 2013 by çì-ỳài

All rights reserved worldwide.

~ ~ ~ *** ~ ~ ~

ISBN: 978-0-9641815-1-9

Also by *çì-ỳàì*

meditations from a servant's dance: give your life 生 *away*

for
l.m.h, my evidence that the Creator exists.

CONTENTS

The moment you were born, a problem was solved.
~ Anonymous

INTRODUCTION

You are today where your thoughts have brought you; you will be tomorrow where your thoughts take you.
~ James Allen

Believe nothing, no matter where you read it, or who said it, even if I have said it, unless it agrees with your own reason and your own common sense.
~ Buddha

The simplest thing cannot be made clear to the most intelligent man if he is firmly persuaded that he knows already, without a shadow of doubt, what is laid before him.
~ Leo Tolstoy

a servant's dance

"MARINE biologist and an actress,*"* stated Jessica.

"Basketball player and a physician," screamed Carmen. "I want to own a sports bar that converts into a night club after hours," answered Jon. "A director on Broadway," yelled Chao. Zoya proclaimed louder, "A lawyer." The entire class erupted into an excited chorus of undecipherable jargon that vaguely resembled human language, in response to their high school teacher's question, "What are you going to do with your life?" Out of the maze of jumbled, high-pitched, and contorted voices came structured and organized words that signaled the return to order. "What is your life's calling?" Mr. Hani uttered in a low, slow, and monotone voice as he glanced around the room at the sea of young faces. The students' voices froze in place as the words in Mr. Hani's question settled in their eager and naive minds; much like an early morning, humidity-induced haze hovers and lingers over a southern river during the dead of summer. For several more minutes, silence floated over the classroom as if the principal had just announced that tweeting would no longer be allowed and that all cell phones would be immediately confiscated and burned. The words "I don't know," spoken by Leslie, a sweet and animated young lady, erupted out of the silence. Other students in a chorus made it known that they, too, had no clue as to their calling in life. Most even ventured to articulate, with slight embarrassment, that they had never considered such a radical question, and admitted that neither their parents nor any other figure of so–called authority had ever posed such an outlandish inquiry. The students—with great pride, confidence, and a skosh of arrogance—proclaimed in a manner that could only be described with the phrase "Ignorance is bliss" that they were not as familiar with the word "calling" as they were with the words "job," "occupation," "profession" or "career."

Hello family. Every generation throughout the ages from time immemorial has sought answers to the confusing, profound, and gnawing questions, "What am I going to do with

8

my life?" "Why am I here?" "What's my purpose?" "What's my calling?" Some find rejuvenation from the exhaustion incurred during their soul-searching expedition for answers to these questions in the sanctity of a job, occupation, career or a business. However, during rejuvenation, most fall into a coma of complacency found in the sanctity of their profession and never fully regain consciousness to continue their search. Some, however—due to a mysterious antidote known only as a lack of fulfillment, satisfaction, and lasting happiness—awake from the coma of complacency and realize that their expedition to discover their life's calling must go on.

I have been waiting here to go with you on your journey to discover what your life is calling you to do and be (your calling). I know you're anxious to begin, but if you don't mind I have a few suggestions before we start. Good! I knew you wouldn't mind.

Suggestion number one: In accordance with Buddha's quote, I don't want you to believe anything in this volume unless it agrees with your own reason and your own common sense.

Suggestion number two: You must leave the attitudes that End God's Occupation (EGO) in your life behind. Such attitudes prevent you from communicating effectively with—and being in connection to—your divinity (God within), whatever you perceive God to be.

The attitudes of the ego are that you derive your self-worth from how much money you have or earn, the house you live in, the car you drive, your career, job, occupation, or profession, the number of Facebook friends you have, how many tweeter followers you have, the people you associate with, years of education, the school you went to, or the latest state-of-the-art electronic devices you own. Another attitude of the ego is that you must pretend to be someone or something that you're not so that others won't discover how afraid and vulnerable you are. Sometimes the ego causes you to be pretentious, arrogant, and fake to fit in or to mask your fears, shame, and short comings. The ego can also cause you to struggle to live up to the standards set by popular culture and others. It forces you to believe that what you know to be true is and you can't be persuaded otherwise, even if it might dramatically improve your life. Finally, the ego also puts up illogical and unnecessary resistance to anything new and provocative.

Take this moment right now to say goodbye to your ego. I'll wait right over there in the corner for you while you say your tearful good-byes. I warn you your ego will be quite upset that you've decided to leave it behind. You see, much like a barnacle on a whale, your ego is attached to you. It thrived with you as you traveled through a lot of perceived good and bad times; therefore it will feel worthless and powerless without you. Your ego doesn't want the friendship to end—it needs you! You can travel much lighter without ego's baggage. Without your ego you'll have a more open, clearer, receptive, and acute mind and therefore you won't run the risk of missing all the important sights, sounds, experiences, and discussions you'll encounter on our journey.

I want you to know I understand that your old friend ego has defined your self-worth for most of your life, and you may feel somewhat strange and undefined in its absence. You may even feel naked, exposed to the world with nothing to cling to. Therefore, it's my sincere hope that you will let the following words replace your ego's attitudes and serve as your new declaration of self-worth as we travel together and even far after our journey together has ended.

I am a divine expression and extension of the Creator. Therefore, I am complete and there is nothing I can do or acquire that will make me more perfect and precious than I am at this very moment.

May you never forget this. Oh, I almost forgot to warn you: even though you've decided to bid your ego a final farewell, there's a possibility—well actually, there's a strong possibility—that it will show up at some point later during our journey. It will appear at certain crucial moments and pretend that it just wanted to say hello or to see how you're doing. It might even bring you a present just to illustrate that it misses you, much like an ex-love interest who wants back into your life (you know the type), or it might be upset with you. Acknowledge your ego when it appears but don't bargain with it, neither explain yourself or your actions to it. Recite your new self-worth mantra until your ex-friend ego is gone. Don't resume your journey through this volume until you can see your ego far off into the horizon moving away from you.

Suggestion number three: Have an open mind to everything you read and experience on this journey and, in accordance with Tolstoy's words, don't be attached to any particular pre-conceived notions about what you will discover.

This small volume flows to you as the result of suffering, resistance, contemplation, meditation, surrender, wisdom, and love.

Whatever you do, or dream you can, begin it.
Boldness has genius and power and magic in it.
~ Johann Wolfgang von Goethe

Let's begin! ~ çì-ỳài

Chapter 1

Give My Life Away?

Let your aim be the good of all.
~ Bhagavad-Gita

*When the world was still new, our common Creator granted
the breath of life alone, but on us he further bestowed
sovereign reason, the impulse to aid one another.*
~ Juvenal

*The purpose of human life is to serve and to show
compassion and the will to help others.*
~ Albert Schweitzer

give your life 生 *away*

AS, she entered the house-fresh from a field trip to the local airport — Stone, a spirited sixteen-year-old, proclaimed proudly and with great enthusiasm, "I'm going to be a pilot, mom."

"I take it you enjoyed the field trip," stated Stone's mom.

"I loved it! It was great! We watched the airplanes take off and land. I couldn't help but wonder where each airplane was going and what the people on them may have been thinking as they boarded their flights. It was exciting to see how some of the passengers were greeted by people who were waiting for them to arrive. The pilots looked so professional in their uniforms mom, and they all looked so happy as they got on and off the airplanes. Mom, you know I have always been fascinated with airplanes, even when I was a little girl. Mom, I want to fly airplanes for a living, please, please, please!"

"Stone, there are no female airline pilots," her mom retorted.

"Well, I'll be the first," stated Stone with confidence.

Immediately and in a soft, swift tone, Stone's mother uttered words that kill dreams. "It might be more practical for you to consider being a stewardess, nurse, or maybe a teacher. I want you to get a good education, a good job, and make a comfortable living."

"But mom, please! This is what I want."

"Stone, I'm your mom and I know what's best for you. I don't want to hear anymore about this pilot stuff."

Stone's mom, without giving any thought at all as to what might be Stone's calling in life, burst the precious bubble that held her daughter's dream of being a pilot. Although her actions were harsh, we can't condemn her because she was also told, without any regard to what might be her calling in life, to go to school, get a good education, get a good job, and make a comfortable living when she as a young woman proclaimed to all the world that she wanted to spend her life as an astronaut. The advice Stone's mom received

13

was revolutionary when we consider that the advice given to females a generation earlier went something like, "Find a man, get married, and have children."

Well, Stone did what she was told to do. She went to college, received a good education, became a terrific nurse, and made a comfortable living. However, as life went on, she found that she was not as content as she had hoped to be. Sure, Stone had some happy times, but she never really experienced any lasting fulfillment or peace. She often felt as though something was missing.

Like so many of us who are discouraged from following our heart and from discovering our calling, Stone settled for a life that was less than satisfying or fulfilling.

"I'm not being ungrateful. We have everything we always hoped for—success, money, home, cars, (and don't forget my membership at the golf club)—but I'm not happy," stated Tyler shamefully to his wife Okelani, as she prepared dinner. "Sweetheart, you know I spent long hours thinking about my purpose in life after listening to that motivational speaker many years ago at the civic center. You remember that retreat that I went on to get in touch with my inner-self?"

"Yes, dear I sure do it was pretty expensive," said Okelani.

"Come on, baby. I'm not talking about the expense; I'm baring my soul here. Be serious! I'm talking about all the soul-searching I put into discovering why I'm here. I read all the self-help and career books. The self-help books told me that I should choose work that I had a passion for and loved so much that I would do the work for free. Although I knew my purpose had to be more significant than having a particular profession or job, I still followed the suggestions in those career books and took tests that determined what occupation I was most qualified for. Do you remember, sweetheart?"

"Yes, darling, I remember," said Okelani in a tone of exhaustion.

"I even asked your dad what he thought my purpose in

life was which was a huge mistake. That was the last time I asked his opinion on anything. I asked close family members, relatives, friends, even strangers. Remember the waiter at the opening of that fancy Chinese restaurant downtown? I asked him what he thought my purpose in life was after I opened a fortune cookie that said, 'Your search is over.' He looked at me as if I had contaminated him with *E. coli.*"

"Anyway, after considering everything I discovered and all the advice I received, I decided that my purpose in life was to create video games. I really thought that was it. I really like the work. I'm very good at it, and the pay is great, but I'm sorry, Lani, I'm not happy or satisfied. Since I feel this way, how could creating video games be my purpose in life? I feel like such a fool after all I went through to discover what I thought was my purpose. Honey, what should I do now?"

In excitement Okelani blurted, "Take my dad's advice and work for him."

"No! Absolutely not," stated Tyler sternly.

"Just kidding, honey. I thought I might interject a little humor into an otherwise downer conversation," stated Okelani, half laughing. "Okay, I'll be serious. I know you're hurting, Tyler. Keep searching, honey. You'll find your purpose, I'm sure of it!"

Why is it difficult for most people to discover their calling in life? As with the high school students mentioned in the introduction, some of us were never taught to think of our lives in terms of having a particular calling, nor were we told to consider why we're here. Therefore, through no fault of our own, we had no reason to pursue our calling. Thus, we got a good education and a good job, or we received no education and went from job to job, or we went from owning one business to owning several throughout our lives, never really experiencing lasting satisfaction, fulfillment, or happiness, even though we may have achieved material wealth.

On the other hand, some of us were taught that our lives derived their significance from what job, career, occupation or business we wanted. Therefore, we equated our calling in life with the pursuit of our profession, and erroneously believed that being busily engaged in that profession was our calling.

As with Stone, some of us were discouraged from following our heart by well-meaning parents who, because of ignorance, tradition, or backward thinking, advised us to take the practical road in life. Most of us who traveled the practical road never discovered our calling. Although some of us achieved monetary and career success on the practical road of life, few if any of us experienced any lasting fulfillment.

Tyler, not unlike a small minority of people, had insight enough to know that, prior to deciding what to do with his life, he should discover his purpose first and that his purpose in life had nothing to do with having a good job, career, or occupation. However, like Tyler and through no fault of their own, most people erroneously seek to discover their purpose from the wrong sources. These wrong sources are books and other literature that equate one's purpose in life with a profession, occupation, or one's passion. Most people, as with Tyler, also erroneously seek advice from family, relatives, friends, and sometimes strangers as to their purpose. They follow this advice, yet remain unhappy, not fully alive or satisfied with life and wondering, "Is this really the reason why I'm here? Is this really my purpose? There must be more to life."

The fact that you exist means that you were created for a reason by something more powerful than yourself, a supreme power or being, the Creator (whatever you perceive the Creator to be). For you to know, for example, why a robot was created, you would not ask the robot; instead, you would have to ask the robot-maker or manufacturer. The robot itself could tell you what tasks it could perform based on the information found in its software, but it couldn't tell you precisely why it was created because it did not create itself. An individual other than the robot-maker or manufacturer could guess intelligently as to why the robot was created, but to obtain the precise reason why the robot was created or manufactured, you would have to ask the maker or manufacturer. Only they would know their intentions or motives for creating the robot.

When you consult any source other than that which created you, it's impossible to receive a precise or exact answer as to why, or for what purpose, you were created. The source would only be guessing or speculating. Simply put, the source did not create you and therefore couldn't possibly know exactly why you're here or what your calling is. Anyone leading a life according to a purpose that they discovered from sources that did not create them, such as self-help books, career guides, family, therapists, spouses, friends, relatives, or strangers, would be leading a life based on speculation rather than the true and precise reason why they were created. Although the information discovered from these sources might be helpful, encouraging, or make you feel good temporarily, because it's based on speculation or intelligent guessing, you would most likely be unable to sustain any real, lasting fulfillment or satisfaction in life by living according to such information.

Therefore, to know the exact answer as to why you were created, you must consult the source that made you (the Creator). Only the Creator can tell you precisely why you were created or what your calling is.

Throughout history the Creator has revealed, and is still revealing today, in Religious, Spiritual, and Philosophical writings why you, the students, Stone, and Tyler were created. The following, as well as those on the first page of this chapter, are just a few excerpts from some of those writings.

The highest of distinctions is service to others.
~ King George VI

And whosoever of you will be the chiefest, shall be servant of all.
~ Bible

Albert Einstein embodied the idealism of service when he was asked,"why are we here?" to which he replied we are here to serve others.
~ Albert Einstein

We came here to serve not be served.
~ Anonymous

*If you want happiness
for an hour – take a nap
If you want happiness
for a day – go fishing.
If you want happiness
for a month – get married.
If you want happiness
for a year – inherit a fortune.
If you want happiness
for a lifetime – help someone else.*
~ Chinese proverb

Rendering help to another is the function of all human beings.
~ Jainism

give your life 生 *away*

*I know of no great man except those who have rendered
great service to the human race.*
~ Voltaire

All men are responsible for one another.
~ Judaism

The greatest quality is seeking to serve others.
~ Buddha

*Be alert to give service – what counts most in life is what
we do for others.*
~ Anonymous

Let no one seek his own good, but the good of his neighbor.
~ Christianity

The best of men are those who are useful to others.
~ Islam

*Independence? That's middle-class blasphemy. We are all
dependent on one another,
every soul of us on earth.*
~ George Bernard Shaw

*Without selfless service are not objectives fulfilled; in
service lies the purest action.*
~ Sikhism
No one has learned the meaning of life until he has

a servant's dance

surrendered his ego to the service of his fellow men.
~ Beran Wolfe

The sage does not accumulate for himself.
The more he uses for others, the more he has himself.
The more he gives to others, the more he possesses of his
own.
~ Taoism

You must live for another if you wish to live for yourself.
~ Seneca

The wise work for the welfare of the world, without thought
to themselves.
~ Hinduism

Guardianship is not to give an order
but to give one's self.
~ African Traditional Religions

The best way to find yourself is to lose yourself in the
service of others.
~ Gandhi

The man of perfect virtue, wishing to be established

20

*himself, seeks also to establish others; wishing to be
enlarged himself, he seeks also to enlarge others.*
~ Confucianism

*Do not seek to benefit only yourself, but think of other
people also.*
~ American Indigenous People Saying

*If I employ others for my own purposes
I myself shall experience servitude,
But if I use myself for the sake of others
I shall experience only lordliness.*
~ Buddhism

An examination of these few, among the many, Religious, Spiritual, and Philosophical writings lead to the inescapable conclusion that the reason you, and all human beings without exception, were created is to help others. You're here to give your life away in service to others. Every individual without exception has the same calling – *to give their lives away in service to humanity.*

Congratulations! You've discovered your life's calling. You've not only discovered your calling, but you've discovered the key to permanent fulfillment, satisfaction, peace, lasting happiness, and prosperity.

Take the time right now, this very moment, to celebrate. Call someone and share. From this moment forward your life will never be the same. Go out to dinner, celebrate enjoy, enjoy, enjoy! Besides, when you return we'll have a lot of work to do.

A thorough examination of nature, our planet, and the universe as evident by the way in which they exist in harmony leads to the inescapable conclusion that their calling is also to serve humanity. When the trees provide oxygen, they're serving us, thereby fulfilling their calling. We serve the trees by the carbon dioxide we provide. The sun serves us by providing, among others things, life-sustaining heat and sunlight.

Not only does our planet serve us by providing life-sustaining provisions such as food and water, it also serves us aesthetically by providing views and vistas of mountains, valleys, and waterways that give us unimaginable serenity. Just think how much tranquility and joy you glean from the sun setting on the ocean, the beauty of the sun cascading on a lake or stream, viewing the awe-inspiring majesty of snowcapped mountains in winter, and witnessing hundreds of blades of grass dancing on the floor of a windswept, lush, beautiful, and prodigious valley. Nature does a spectacular job serving us in extraordinary ways. The universe—consisting of the stars, moon, and the planets—serve us by providing a nightly show of spectacular beauty and a magnificent backdrop in which to dream or to carry on a romantic encounter.

Giving your life away in service to others is the highest expression of yourself. It is the ultimate expression of love, the love from which each person was created. You give your life away in service to others by throwing your whole heart, soul, and energy into doing all you can to help improve the condition of humanity.

Although every individual has the same calling (to give their lives away in service to humanity), we each perform our calling differently by using our own individual unique Creator – given talent to do so.

For every Creator—given unique talent that each person possesses—there are corresponding needs of individuals in the world waiting to be served by the use of those unique talents.

Therefore, all individuals must use their unique talent to fulfill the corresponding unique need of humanity that their unique talent was given to them to fulfill. Because your particular talent is unique to you and no one else on the planet has it, if you do not use it to fulfill the unique need of humanity for your unique talent, that need of humanity will, tragically for humankind, not be served. Just think, there are people in the world with needs waiting to be served by you through the use of your unique talent. Doesn't the thought of that make you feel powerful, humble, and thankful?

Just for a moment, try to recall how exuberant it felt to do something loving, helpful, and kind for someone—especially something that comes natural to you. Remember how loved the person you were helping felt, how grateful and happy they were? Do you remember how exalted you felt, a feeling of euphoria, love, and fulfillment that you couldn't describe? Remember how the people around you felt, their faces lit up with joy even though they themselves weren't the subject of your service? That is the power and majesty of service, unlike the happy feelings you sometimes get from societal rewards (material possessions, power, and recognition) which are nice, but temporary and rarely fulfilling.

Recall how wonderful you felt when you witnessed someone doing a loving kind act for someone else, and although you were not the intended subject of the service, you were very much emotionally affected in a beautiful way by it. The joy, love, and happiness experienced from service is contagious.

There is nothing on earth that a person could do that would bring them staggering joy, majestic peace, and prodigious love than giving their life away in service to others.

Experiencing the splendor of permanent—not temporary—fulfillment and satisfaction, lasting happiness, love, and prosperity is the unintended gift that is yours for giving your life away in service to humanity.

Chapter 2

What Does It Mean To Serve Humanity?

He is great who confers the most benefits.
~ Ralph Waldo Emerson

Past the seeker as he prayed came the crippled and the beggar and the beaten. And seeing them... he cried, "Great God, how is it that a loving creator can see such things and yet do nothing about them?" God said, "I did do something. I made you."
~ Anonymous

To give pleasure to a single heart by a single kind act is better than a thousand head-bowings in prayer.
~ Saadi

give your life 生 *away*

SINGING – "I'm cool, I'm cool, I'm the coolest dude in school. I'm cute, I'm cute, up here in my altar suit. I'm smart, I'm smart, lighting these candles is an art." The Pastor makes the "Shh! Shh!" noise as he raises his pointer finger to his lips. I had been singing and talking out loud again, Charles thought to himself, *but at least this time I hadn't uttered any filthy words. It's cool being an acolyte, helping God and Pastor up here at the altar. My classmates are so jealous. I get to leave class early and return late. Hallelujah! Little ole me, all four feet ten inches of me, God's helper! How could that be, me a helper of God? I've never actually given God anything to eat or drink. Well, there was that one time that I mistakenly laid my tuna sandwich and juice box on the altar, but I removed it so quickly as to cover up my mistake, that I don't think God had time to take a bite or a sip. After that, how could I call myself a helper of God? Besides, he has never even bossed me around, like mama does when I help her in the garden.*

"Pastor!" young Charles called out as they both descended the altar in the direction of the Pastor's office. In a very cautious voice he continued, "Am I God's helper? Well, what I really meant to say is what does it mean to be God's helper?"

Pastor takes his glasses from his eyes and rubs them. Anyone that knows Pastor knows that this act signals a moment of contemplation with several minutes of profound pontificating to follow. Charles was really hungry and was regretting having asked such a question, as most of the young kids did back then when Pastor went into protracted discussions on very perplexing and profound issues. "Actually, you are God; we'll talk about that when you get older." Stated Pastor. "Yes!" Pastor uttered with great furor. "You're God's helper, but more importantly a helper of God is actually a servant.

You're a servant to our congregation. You serve the congregation when you help them. Charles, you help the

25

If you give even a cup of cold water to one of the least of my followers, you will surely be rewarded.
~ Bible

congregation each time you light those candles because by doing so you acknowledge the presence of God in our church. You also remind the congregation of God's presence in their lives. When people are reminded of God's presence, they are more inclined to seek God's help. The Creator likes nothing more than when people seek the Creator's help."

"Thanks, Pastor," stated Charles in a half-ungrateful tone, not ungrateful for the answer, but for the time it took Pastor to respond. Young Charles had secretly hoped to shoot a few baskets before returning late to his fifth-grade class to be among his now lowly peers after having been knighted and raised to sainthood when Pastor proclaimed to all the world that he was helper of God, servant of the congregation.

"Where's Baby Kyle?" Stone asked.

"He passed away last night! He passed away in my arms," Misaki stated in a low, slow, and sad voice. "He raised his small egg-sized head, looked at me through his pea-sized eyes, and after a short gasp that his underdeveloped lungs could barely muster, his small, less-than-two-pound body fell limb. No matter how many premature babies pass away on our unit, a part of my soul goes with them. I sat with the parents, hugged them and cried with them as we deliberated in silence the significance Baby Kyle's short life had played in our lives, and how the passing had stung and staggered us. You know me, Stone. No matter how sick the children are, I always foolishly believe that somehow they're going to survive."

"Misaki!" Stone stated softly, "have you been here all night. Did you eat?"

"Yes!" stated Misaki with exhaustion.

"Misaki, you have to stop getting so emotionally involved with every patient. You take each death so hard."

"Don't tell me that! I know you mean well, but you must realize this is what I do. I do this work, well not work, because it's what I live for. I can't help getting so emotional. Although there's sorrow here, I love what I do.

*The race of mankind would perish
did they cease to aid each other.
We cannot exist without mutual help.
All therefore that need aid have a right to ask it from their
fellow-men; and no one who has power of granting can
refuse it without guilt.*
~ Walter Scott

It gives me great joy when I can help by extending my love and professional attention, as a nurse, to these babies. It's the least that I can do to help these young souls and their parents."

"Go home, Misaki. You've been here for over 36 hours."

"Girl I'm tired; in fact, I am exhausted. I'll see you later!" Misaki stated as she gathered her things and proceeded toward the elevator.

"Could you please send up Anderson?"

A 6-foot, 6-inch man built like a military-issued Hummer ascended the stairs of the jail and squeezed himself into the petite, poorly ventilated, smelly, interview booth.

"Hello, Mr. Anderson. My name is Pom. I'm your public defender. I understand that you were arrested and charged with possession of crack cocaine with the intent to distribute. The police found fifteen hits of crack on you. Tell me what happened."

"It wasn't my crack. I didn't do anything wrong. I'm innocent."

"Yeah! Everyone in here is innocent," remarked Pom in a sarcastic tone.

"I can't help you unless you tell me the truth. Now tell me what happened and I won't ask you again. If you don't tell me right now what happened, I won't be back for another month and your bail hearing will be delayed. Do you want that to happen?" Pom, who stood just 5' 2"and weighed no more than the average petite-sized woman, was by any stretch of the imagination a small man that didn't warrant being afraid of, but his words resonated with his clients as if they were spoken by a giant saber tooth tiger with saliva dripping from his huge, vicious, terrifying canine teeth.

"Alright, I'll tell you what happened."

After hearing Anderson's story, which indicated that not only was he guilty as charged but that he also had a crack-cocaine and heroin addiction, Pom sought an explanation as to when and how Anderson had become an addict. The

People are always looking to the Creator for help.
The Creator is looking to people too help.
~ Anonymous

puzzled and baffled expression on Anderson's face indicated that he was surprised and confused by his lawyer's personal interest in his life. You see, in all the years that Anderson had dealt with lawyers and the criminal justice system, no one had ever expressed an interest in his life, especially his drug addiction. "I'm more concerned about you kicking your drug habit than I am about the criminal charges that you're facing."

"Why?" stated Anderson in a bewildered tone.

"Even if I convince a jury not to convict you on these charges, if you don't kick your habit you'll eventually be incarcerated for a long time, die of an overdose, or be killed. This may sound corny to you but, although I'm a lawyer, I consider myself a servant of the people who cares more about his clients' lives than their legal woes."

"I'm here to help you Anderson, first and foremost with your drug habit and what I perceive to be low self-worth. In my opinion, this is what has led you to make bad choices in your life. I need a commitment from you right now that you're going to kick your habit and improve your self-worth!"

Anderson, after several minutes of contemplation and more than a few tears, agreed that after thirteen years of being in an out of jail and a junkie, it was time to kick his habit. He also admitted that he felt worthless and dead inside, and wanted to find a way to somehow get well and feel alive again. As a result of Anderson's commitment to participate in a drug rehabilitation program, Pom was successful in getting probation for him on his charges. Pom also recommended several books and a counseling program that could help Anderson improve his self-worth.

Several months later, Pom was reprimanded by his superiors for sloppy work on some of his clients' cases. Pom had on several other occasions addressed his clients' life issues to the neglect of their legal troubles. He would spend more hours with his clients than were necessary providing

*Man becomes great exactly in the degree to which he works
for the welfare of his fellow man.*
~ Mahatma Gandhi

wise counsel rather than legal advice.

Pom, although a very skilled attorney, was the first to admit that the reprimand was warranted. He realized that although he was a lawyer, he was powerless to stop himself from focusing on his clients' life choices rather than their legal challenges. He knew that his natural inclination was to help his clients not as a lawyer, but as some sort of life counselor. Pom eventually resigned his position with the public defender's office rather than face the inevitable firing.

We serve humanity when we lovingly perform acts that help, benefit, aid, assist or fulfill the needs of others without the expectation of receiving anything in return not even a thank-you. Therefore, you must ask yourself the "I" questions, "How can I help?" "What can I do for them?" "What do I have that they need?" "How can I be of service?" Instead of asking the "Me" questions, "What's in it for me?" "How much will you pay me?" "What can they do for me in return?" "Why won't they help me?"

Those who understand and accept that their reason for being here is to serve realize that this life is not about them, but about serving others. If this existence was about the needs of the individual, then each person would have been created to live in isolation, be self-sufficient, and do things only to please themselves. (Has your ego returned?)

The opposite is true. We were all placed on this planet quite close together with needs that in most cases can't be met without the help or assistance of others. Maybe the next existence will be about the individual; however, this life is about serving others.

Because this life is not about the individual doesn't mean that you can't thoroughly enjoy your life. Service to others is the highest expression of yourself. It is the ultimate expression of love, the love from which each person was created.

Those who give their lives away in service will testify that a life of service provides the highest level of living you can experience—not just wealth, power or recognition, but a more exalted, noble, and glorious, level of living, a living that allows you to enjoy the unintended gifts of permanent fulfillment, satisfaction, ecstasy, peace, prosperity, and joy. It is a miracle that this life is about serving others because it is only through service to others that we enjoy such beautiful unintended gifts. Therefore, when we serve others we immeasurably serve ourselves.

Do we have free will when it has been predetermined that the reason we're here and our calling is to serve humanity? We have the free will to live our lives the way we choose. We can choose to give our lives away in service to humanity or not. However, the unintended gifts and benefits of a life dedicated to service far exceed those of a life devoted to societal rewards (material possessions, power, and recognition).

Charles's lighting of the candles was service to the congregation, and in turn, service to humanity because it was helpful, useful, and beneficial to the congregation to be reminded of the presence of God in their church and in their lives.

Misaki served her infant patients, their parents and, in turn, humanity, by passionately caring for and comforting the infants and their parents during a very difficult and sad period. Misaki's tender, loving professional attention for the infants and their families went above and beyond her duties as a nurse.

Pom—despite jeopardizing his legal career—served his clients and, in turn, humanity, by providing wise counsel which proved more helpful and beneficial than his legal assistance.

As you may have gathered from the actions of Charles, Misaki, and Pom, there are as many different individual unique ways to give your life away in service to humanity as there are people on the planet. The great news is that it only requires simple, helpful, loving, genuine, and sincere action, and in most cases very little effort to serve others.

It was intended that service be easy and rewarding for two reasons. First, life is not supposed to be a burden, but a joy. Secondly, because it's every individual's calling to serve, by making it easy, everyone is assured the opportunity to fulfill their calling and enjoy the unintended gifts.

Serving others can be as simple as smiling at someone. When we smile at someone, our smile—in most cases—is helpful or beneficial in either lifting that person's spirits or bringing out their joy. A silent prayer for someone that crosses your mind or your path, or a random act of kindness such as changing a stranger's flat tire, are very simple, yet powerful, ways to serve others. Serving humanity can also be as complicated as finding a cure for Alzheimer's, advocating the end to human trafficking, teaching new parents parenting skills or creating a device that allows an amputee to live a better and fuller life. However, oftentimes the most loving and helpful act of service we can do for others is to tell them "No" when their real need would not be met or their problem solved by giving them what they want.

Simply, ***when you help others, without the expectation of receiving anything in return, not even a thank-you, you're serving humanity and thereby living and fulfilling your calling.***

The unintended reward for everyday acts of service (as with Charles) is a feeling of purpose, fulfillment, satisfaction, and joy. However, the unintended gifts for a life devoted to service (as with Misaki and Pom), expressed through the use of your Creator-given unique talent, among many, are free and joyous expression of your divinity, permanent fulfillment and satisfaction, prosperity, and lasting happiness.

I was hungered, and ye gave me meat:
I was thirsty, and ye gave me drink:
I was a stranger, and ye took me in:
I was naked, and ye clothed me:
I was sick, and ye visited me:
I was in prison, and ye came unto me.
~ Anon

Chapter 3

How Do I Serve Humanity?

*The person born with a talent they are meant to use will
find their greatest happiness in using it.*
~ Johann Wolfgang von Goethe

*There are different abilities to perform services, but the
same God gives ability to all for their particular service.*
~ Bible

*The Creator has not likened us to the Creator's image with
a calling to carryout to which the Creator did not give us
the ability!*
~ Ha-kim

"THAT was the most fabulous, spectacular, dazzling, and opulent meal that I've ever had the amazing privilege of eating, and I've eaten at the finest restaurants on the globe," Nuying remarked. She had just eaten a meal prepared by Liv—a great friend, confidant, and perhaps the most talented chef the world didn't know. "The crab cakes were sumptuous, marvelously lumpy, and luxuriously seasoned to perfection," Nuying continued with dramatic flair. "The string beans tasted as if they were picked by angels from the Garden of Eden and seasoned with just a hint of nectar from the gods. They burst with magic and excitement on my tongue as they danced smoothly down into my deeply appreciative tummy. I want you to know that life is no longer worth living after eating a slice of your sensational and astonishing coconut cake because I know that I could search the earth for the rest of my days and would have a better chance of finding a teardrop in the Atlantic Ocean before I would find a coconut cake with such a scared, seductive, and mouthwatering taste as the one you prepared with your heavenly hands."

Nuying took a jerky over-developed curtsy (much like the one she took as a little girl after performing her one-girl play during thanksgiving gatherings) as if she had just received a standing ovation for a dramatic performance in *The Taming of the Shrew*, directed by Shakespeare himself. Obviously, Nuying has a flair for the dramatic. She's a breathing, walking, talking dramatization.

Nuying's glowing dramatic tribute was the answer to Liv's perennial prayer; she always questioned whether she was talented enough to be a professional chef. She could not have imagined that the answer to her prayer would have been presented in a fashion that would make the most renowned chef blush. Liv secretly believed, since she was a little girl preparing food for the neighborhood kids on a her Easy Bake Oven, that although there were many fine cooks in the world, she prepared meals in her own unique way, better than anyone on the planet. Her belief was now backed

give your life 生 *away*

Everyone according to their talent and every talent according to its work.
~ French Proverb

by Nuying's highest dramatic theatrical approval.

As a closet chef, Liv planned to one day prepare and serve exquisite meals to customers assembled in her very own five-star restaurant, once retired from her job as senior vice president of a software company.

"Sweetheart, Dr. Ali is a phenomenal instructor. He explains International Law so well that even a child would understand. What I really enjoy, though, is how he weaves his work and life experience into his lectures and class discussions. The best part is that he finds a way to give great, sage-like advice on profound, life-changing issues. That's where he really shines," Yukio, a passionate graduate student, stated to his wife Noni.

Dr. Ali is a humble man with a glowing personality who puts his entire heart and soul into his penetrating and compelling lectures, like the one he gave his mother when he was only three scolding her about how could she pout and not speak to the family, after a particular incident, if she was really the religious person she claimed to be.

Dr. Ali has an astonishing ability of helping you feel great about your life, even when you're feeling disheartened, and compelling and empowering you to take action to improve your outlook. He often thought to himself that his unique way of teaching and giving life-changing advice to others was a gift from the Creator. In fact, he secretly believed that he gave wise counsel to others, in his unique way, better than anyone else in the world. However, his humility pre-empted him from ever publicly making such a proclamation.

Dr. Ali was hesitant to share his talent with others beyond his inner circle, or the classroom, for fear of being labeled a motivational or inspirational speaker. He believed that the spell cast over audiences by such speakers often wore off long before the audience members would take action in their lives. He felt strongly that wise counsel had to be delivered in such a powerful and practical manner as to compel and empower people to act, and to act decisively.

give your life 生 away

Whatever you are by nature, keep to it;
never desert your line of talent.
Be what nature intended you for,
and you will succeed.
~ Sydney Smith

Although everyone has the same calling to serve humanity, each person was given a unique ability to perform their service in a way different than anyone else. Your unique ability to perform your service is your Creator-given talent. Every person, without exception—regardless of race, religion, sex, sexual orientation, country of residence, socio-economic status, height, weight, level of physical mobility, or mental acuity—was blessed with a Creator-given, unique talent. If you feel as though you don't have such a talent that only means that you haven't discovered it yet. We'll work on your discovery in the next chapter.

Your unique talent is a divinely endowed ability that you received the moment you came into existence. This talent exists in the form of a unique, creative, and/or artistic aptitude. You might be thinking that you have many talents, and you probably do. However, of the talents that you possess, you have one ability that allows you to do a certain thing, in the way that you do it, better than anyone else, who *has* lived, *is* living, or who *will ever live*. That ability is your unique talent. Yes, that's right! You do one thing, in the way that you do it, better than anyone else in history. No one else on the planet can do that one thing better than you! That's powerful! Only you possess this unique talent.

Your DNA suggests just how unique you are. There is no one who has *lived*, is *living*, or who will ever *live*, that had, has, or will have your exact DNA. You're an original without a copy.

Nuying, Liv, and Dr. Ali were each given a unique talent to use to serve others. They have all been using their unique talent to serve others since they were very young, although they were not fully aware or conscious of it.

You can infer from the way Nuying drooled with her words while describing the meal prepared by Liv that she has a tremendous love for the spoken word, along with an immense flair for the dramatic, although she spends her days as a newspaper columnist.

give your life 生 *away*

Everyman loves what they are good at.
~ Anonymous

Nuying is a closet actress. It's her dirty little secret; her parents would be appalled if she quit her "good job" to be an actress. That would be scandalous! It's apparent that Nuying, although a very talented writer, has a unique talent for dramatic acting.

Based on Liv's secret thoughts about her cooking and Nuying's enthusiastic, dramatic confirmation of those thoughts, it's clear that Liv's unique talent is her cooking ability.

It's evident from Yukio's glowing remarks to his wife, and from Dr. Ali's own belief in himself, that Dr. Ali's unique talent is his ability to deliver sagacious, penetrating, life-altering guidance that not only motivates and inspires but compels and empowers people to act.

When Nuying is writing her column, Liv is performing her duties as a V.P., and Dr. Ali is teaching, they are performing their jobs with the intention of receiving a benefit in return, usually money.

When you perform a job with the intention of receiving certain benefits (money, power, and recognition), these benefits will usually appear in your life. Some people are satisfied with them while other's aren't; they're left unfulfilled, thinking that there must be more to life.

It's through conscious service to others, while using your unique talent, without the expectation of receiving anything in return, not even a thank-you, that you will experience permanent fulfillment, lasting happiness, and true prosperity.

When you intentionally use that ability that allows you to do one thing better than anyone on the planet to help others you're using your unique talent to serve humanity and thereby living and fulfilling your calling.

Nuying's calling to serve others through the use of her unique talent for dramatic acting would be achieved by becoming an actor. Her acting would meet the needs of those who seek inspiration and motivation from the arts and those who secretly hold dreams of making their very own acting

give your life 生 *away*

Hide not your talents,
they for use were made,
what's a sun-dial in the shade!
~ Benjamin Franklin

debut. Great acting has always inspired and motivated the young and old to dream, and sometimes plot a new course in life.

Liv's calling to serve others through the use of her unique talent for cooking would be achieved by opening her very own five-star restaurant. Her cooking and restaurant would meet the needs of those who seek to revel in the tastes and smells of a delectable mouthwatering meal served in an opulent space.

Dr. Ali's calling to serve others through the use of his unique talent for giving compelling, sagacious, life-altering guidance would be achieved by becoming a public lecturer and speaker. His lecturing and speaking would meet the needs of those all over the world who crave, hunger, and thirst for wise, penetrating, and life-changing guidance.

As you seek to serve humanity and journey to discover your unique talent, the way you look at things will change. You will discover that the calling to give your life away in service to humanity will be more desirable than a life simply devoted to a job, career, occupation or success. You will no longer contemplate what kind of job, occupation, or career you want and the rewards that come with them (material possessions, power, recognition) because they will no longer appeal to you. Instead, your first priority will be to seek opportunities to use your unique talent to help others and to improve the condition of humankind. You will experience your higher self (being loved and giving love) and the permanent spiritual gifts that come with that (peace, joy, fulfillment, and prosperity) as you give your life away in service to humanity.

As you use your unique talent to serve others, you will be stunned by how natural, effortless, and fun your calling is. You will also be delighted by the abundance generated from the use of your unique talent; that will manifest itself in your life and in the lives of others.

No unique talent is more or less significant than any

give your life 生 *away*

Your unique talent is the Creator's gift to you.
What you do with it is your gift to humanity.
~ Ha-kim

other; all are equally precious to the Creator and desperately needed by humanity. Just because your unique talent is parenting doesn't make it less significant than someone whose unique talent is neurosurgery. Each individual's unique talent is a divine expression of the Creator and therefore equal to any other.

When you use your unique talent to serve others, you're living in your most natural state and are a phenomenal expression of divinity. You need only to discover your unique talent and then have the courage to spend your life using that talent to serve humanity.

Chapter 4

How Do I Discover My Unique Talent?

Silence is the language of God.
~ Swami Sivanada

In the attitude of silence the soul finds the path in a clearer light, and what is elusive and deceptive resolves itself into crystal clearness.
~ Gandhi

Be still and know that I am God!
~ Bible

"DON'T do that Skye! You might hurt yourself Skye, you can't do that."

"Why not?" stated Skye abruptly.

"Because I said so! Skye, please sit still; you're driving me crazy. You're not old enough to do that yet. You're smaller than the others kids. Wait until you grow up to try that. Why can't you be more like your brother? Why can't you be more like your sister? You can't do anything right. Why can't you be more like your cousin Beth? You're just like your lazy father. You're just like your angry and bitter mother."

Skye recalled the voices of her youth as she sat near the calming waters of a river that ran through breathtaking Yosemite National Park. As she introduced her feet to the river's freezing cold, crystal clear, running water, her body recoiled. Undeterred by the water's frigid temperature, she continued in deep thought and reflection on how she had arrived at her current station in life.

"Skye, my dear, you should be an accountant; you're excellent at math. It's a really hot field and you can make a good living." Skye recalled a conversation with her mother when she was choosing a career. "But I really want to be a deep sea diver," Skye protested. "That's my dream, mom."

"That's not practical! Girls don't do those things. Besides, you want to get a good education in a field that's hiring, so you can get a good job and be of service to others."

"Maybe you're right; I suppose deep sea diving is a pretty silly idea for a girl." Skye got a degree in accounting and a "good job" with great pay. She married a "great guy" and had three children, but it turned out that she was not the only woman her great guy was great to. In time, she divorced her "great guy."

Although Skye's career provided her with material wealth, notoriety, and the ability to serve others, she found herself, after her children had reached adulthood, sitting on the banks of the river contemplating that all too familiar

Silence is when we hear inwardly;
sound, when we hear outwardly.
~ Thoreau

feeling—that something was missing, and wondering why she felt unfulfilled.

Why didn't Skye follow her heart and become a deep sea diver? Because Skye, like most of us at an early time in our lives, wasn't allowed to become who the Creator created her to be.

Our well-meaning parents or loved ones often suffocated our desires that would've lead to the discovery of our unique talent by telling us what to do and what not to do. They did this instead of letting us freely discover our unique talent and who we were intended to be.

Parents—along with family, the church, the community, friends, popular culture, and society—shaped us with the best intentions (or in some cases, maybe not the best intentions) into what they believed we should be. After years of this type of influence, we neglect to discover our unique talent, and we become someone other than the person that we were intended to be.

If the influential forces in your early life would've been patient with your development and nurtured your true essence you might've discovered, for example, that you would've been happiest and fulfilled as a roller coaster designer as opposed to a stockbroker. Maybe you would've discovered that you had a unique talent for robotics and therefore should serve humanity as a scientist or engineer as opposed to being a senator just because you were born in a family with a long history of political service. Come close so that you can hear what I'm about to say. Are you close? Please don't blame anyone. The people that influenced your life were, in most cases, well-meaning with honorable intentions. They did to you, with the best intentions, what was done to them with the best intentions. Blame them for nothing and forgive them for everything. The forgiveness is not for them; it's for you. It releases you from the past to be free to enjoy the present, and to move peacefully into the future. Now, I want you to forgive yourself for the so-called bad choices you think you made in your life that prevented you from discovering your unique talent and from becoming who you were intended to be. Now that all the necessary forgiveness has taken place, let's begin the discovery of your unique talent.

Unlike the discovery of your calling you don't have to consult the Creator to discover your unique talent. In order for you, as with Skye, to discover your unique talent, you must make a journey of introspection. As mentioned earlier, the moment you came into existence, you received an ability, unique only to you, to fulfill your calling. Therefore, the discovery of that ability (unique talent) begins and ends with your soul. The soul is that part of the Creator's spirit that went into making you. Its language is silence, and it only speaks when there is silence; it will not compete with any noise from anyone or anything. Consequently, for you to make an effective and rewarding journey of introspection, you must banish the external noise (noise heard by the ears) and internal noise (thoughts in your mind) and replace them with external and internal silence. Mother Teresa and Swami Sivanada said it best.

We cannot put ourselves directly in the presence of God if
we do not practice internal and external silence.
~ Mother Teresa

Silence is the language of God.
~ Swami Sivanada

Meditation is the action of silence.
~ Krishnamurti

Once the internal and external noise is banished, it will be in the unexpected moments of external and internal silence that you will have the amazing privilege and pleasure of hearing the exalted voice of your soul and listening to the sublime, miraculous revelation as to what unique talent you possess.

It's very difficult to banish the external and internal noise and, in turn, hear the voice of our souls. That's because we lead excessively busy and noisy lives. When you're in your car, at work, or at home, you're exposed to noises from the cell phone, home phone, office phone, Blackberry, laptop, internet, iPod, iPad, car radio, DVD player, television, co-workers, boss, children, spouse, relatives, friends, pets, neighbors, lawn mower, blower, and a host of other things.

To banish the external noise, you must find a quiet space where you can be alone with yourself. Find a quiet retreat like a park, resort, a cabin by the ocean or a lake, or any peaceful place in nature. Electronic devices, with the exception of maybe a cell phone to be used only in an emergency, are not allowed.

The reflective and sagacious—to name a few, Jesus, Muhammad, and Buddha—sought the Creator in the silence and solitude of the mountains, desert, and forest.

If you can't afford to retreat to nature, although you really can't afford not to, try finding quiet and silence at home. To find quiet and silence at home, you must take time away from your everydayness, work, electronic devices, visitors, friends, and family. Send the children and the spouse away.

No matter what physical space you discover is the best environment for you to banish your external noise, you will encounter a strong temptation to reclaim some noise as a measure of comfort. Resist the temptation. In time, it will pass; be strong. You've lived with noise for so long that noise, like your ego, has become a great friend and a comfort in your life. It won't leave you without being forced to do so.

Finding your quiet space and residing there in silence

Silence is the language of the soul;
the soul is that part of the Creator's spirit
that went into making you.
~ Ha-kim

will end the external noise.

After the external noise has been banished, you'll have the internal noise in your mind that remains—noise from echoes of past memories or conversations, noise from present thoughts of worry, fear, work, something you forgot to do, have to do, or noise from thoughts of plans or concerns for the future. Banishing internal noise in your life is similar to quieting a large crowd; the larger and louder the crowd, the longer it takes to silence it. Therefore, the louder and more extensive your internal noise, the longer it will take to banish it. Be patient! You'll banish it and achieve internal silence.

Here it comes. You've heard it stated a quadrillion times before: The best, easiest, and quickest way to banish your old friend internal noise is to meditate while you're in your quiet space. Meditation will quiet your body, your mind, and more importantly your soul. Meditation allows you to go from a noisy mind, to a mind that concentrates on a few key thoughts, to a mind that is empty of any thoughts (nothingness). It will take practice to reach the state where your mind is absent of any thoughts, but again be patient. You will reach it, not necessarily when you want to, but exactly when you should.

There are hundreds of books and digital media available on how to properly meditate. You'll find that because meditation is so beneficial, you'll want to incorporate it into your daily life long after you discover your unique talent.

When, as the result of silence and meditation, you reach a state of nothingness, (no sound or thought) you've banished both external and internal noise. At first, it will only be for a short time that you'll experience a state of nothingness, but as you get better at meditating, the time will increase.

Once in a state of silence and nothingness for a reasonable period of time (as determined by you), introduce thoughts which help you recall what you dreamed of doing when you were younger, what you dream of doing now, what you think you do in the way that you do it better than anyone else in the

In prayerful silence you must look into your own heart.
No one can tell you better than yourself what comes
between you and God. Ask yourself. Then listen!
~ Johannes Tauler

world, what you have been doing all your life—on and off in bits and pieces—that is natural and effortless for you, when you're doing it you get lost in time, it gives you fulfillment, but you never attempted to make a living at it.

Maybe, when you were younger, you dreamed of building furniture. You still dream of building furniture; the desire has never really left you. You believe that you build furniture in your own way, better than anyone else on the planet. You've been thinking about and tinkering with furniture, on and off for most of your life. You built furniture for your tree house when you were growing up. Your interest and talent for furniture-building is natural and effortless, when you build furniture you get lost in time but you never took the step to build furniture for a living. You love sharing your interest in furniture—building with others. You would probably build furniture for free and give it away if you could afford to do so.

Maybe, when you were younger, you dreamed of writing plays. You still dream of writing plays; the desire has never really left you. You believe that you write plays, in your own way, better than anyone else in the world. You've been writing plays on and off, in bits and pieces, most of your life. You wrote them as a child and had the neighborhood children perform them. Writing plays is natural and effortless for you, you get lost in time when you write plays but you never took the step to write plays for a living. You love sharing your plays with others. You would probably write plays for free if you could afford to do so.

Why introduce these thoughts into a state of silence and nothingness? The introduction of a pebble into a raging river will produce little to no effect, but the introduction of a pebble into a still pond will produce many ripples. A thought introduced into a noisy mind produces little to no effect. A thought introduced into a silent and still mind produces amazing and miraculous results.

Let the thoughts that you introduced into your state of

The voice of the soul competes not with noise;
it utters its wisdom in its native tongue, silence!
~ Ha-kim

silence marinate in your soul. Return once again to a state of silence and nothingness and then ask yourself the following question: *If I were sentenced to give my life away in service to humanity for an eternity, in what unique way would I perform my service?*

The question is now safely within the confines of your soul, and your soul will decide the perfect time to answer. Have no preconceived notions as to what the answer will be or when you'll receive it. The answer may come while you're in the shower, driving, or while you're sleeping. Trust your divinity. The answer may not come when you want it, but it will be on time.

You will know that your soul has answered your question when you hear your internal silent voice (the soul speaks to you in your own voice, not the voice Moses heard on the mountain top from the burning bush) in its truthful, calm, and peaceful tone, tell you what your unique talent is and your reaction to that answer is a feeling of love, euphoria, and peace. In most cases, if you don't react with feelings of love and euphoria when you hear what your unique talent is, that probably means that your mind has taken up the call to discover your unique talent. But understand it's not in the mind where the answer lies but in the soul. The feelings of love and euphoria are simply confirmation from the soul that you have indeed discovered your Creator-given, unique talent.

You'll probably have to repeat the process of banishing external and internal noise several times before your soul reveals what your unique talent is. Each person's discovery is different, yet similar. Be patient!

Although no one can discover your unique talent for you, I can give you a hint. Generally, your unique talent is something that you've been doing most of your life, that you're great at which is natural and is effortless for you— something you are passionate about and want to share with others. It also gives a you sense of purpose, joy, and lasting fulfillment.

Once you discover your unique talent, it would be a good idea to put it in a *calling statement* similar to the example provided below.

Example of a person with a unique talent for cooking:

I will give my life away in service to humanity, without the expectation of receiving anything in return, not even a thank-you, by using my (your unique talent example – <u>cooking skills</u>), to (describe the help you'll provide – <u>cook nutritional meals for school children</u>).

The following examples are provided to assist you in being as thorough as possible in creating your *calling statement*. It should be short and simple. Read it often; it will keep you on your calling.

Example of a calling statement for a person with a unique talent for painting:

I will give my life away in service to humanity, without the expectation of receiving anything in return, not even a thank-you, by using my painting skills to paint exquisite, amazing, inspiring, and captivating landscapes.

Example of a calling statement for a person with a unique talent for imparting knowledge to children:

I will give my life away in service to humanity, without the expectation of receiving anything in return, not even a thank-you, by using my instructional skills to share my knowledge and life experiences with students, while motivating, educating, and encouraging them.

Example of a calling statement for a person with a unique talent for caring for the sick, injured, or the dying:

I will give my life away in service to humanity, without the expectation of receiving anything in return, not even a thank-you, by using my health care skills to travel in my mobile home to treat the sick, injured, or the dying wherever I find them.

Example of a calling statement for a person with a unique talent for planning:

I will give my life away in service to humanity, without the expectation of receiving anything in return, not even a thank-you, by using my planning skills, to plan events that are creative, uplifting, beneficial, and a blast.

Example of a calling statement for a person who has a unique talent for engaging others in conversation:

I will give my life away in service to humanity, without the expectation of receiving anything in return, not even a thank-you, by using my conversational skills to host programs or shows that discuss significant, progressive, insightful, provocative, and life-changing issues.

Example of a calling statement for a person with a unique talent for creating musical arrangements:

I will give my life away in service to humanity, without the expectation of receiving anything in return, not even a thank-you, by using my composition skills to write music that is sublime, beautiful, and illuminating.

Example of a calling statement for a person with the unique talent for advocating for the rights of the less fortunate:

I will give my life away in service to humanity, without the expectation of receiving anything in return, not even a thank-you, by using my advocacy skills to advocate for human rights and basic necessities (food, water, shelter, work, dignity, education, and security) for the powerless and the voiceless.

Now that you've discovered your unique talent and put it into a calling statement, it's up to you to make your calling statement a reality. Start serving humanity by using your unique talent and experience the magnificent unintended benefits.

I bet you thought I forgot about Skye. No way! Skye discovered that her unique talent was in fact deep sea diving—it always had been. Although she was an accountant, she maintained a keen interest in deep sea diving by frequently diving and keeping abreast of the latest deep sea diving equipment, advancements, and technology.

After Skye decided to give her life away in service through the expression of her newly discovered unique talent that nagging feeling of not being fulfilled and wondering if there was more to life disappeared.

Here's Skye's calling statement.

I will give my life away in service to humanity, without the expectation of receiving anything in return, not even a thank-you, by using my deep sea diving skills for scientific purposes to help preserve the oceans, marine life, and the planet.

Chapter 5

How Do I Conquer The Fear Of Giving My Life Away?

Nothing in life is to be feared.
It is only to be understood.
~ Marie Curie

What is needed, rather than running away or controlling
or suppressing or any other resistance is understanding
fear; that means, watch it, learn about it, come directly
into contact with it. We are to learn about fear, not how to
escape from it.
~ Krishnamurti

Fear knocked at the door. Love and courage answered.
Nothing was there.
~ Ha-kim

"*HELLO*, may I speak to Kairo?"

"Kairo, there's someone on the phone for you."

"Hi, Kairo. This is Milstein. How are you?"

"I am doing fine."

"How would you like your old job back? I know the layoff was tough, but the company is in the process of rehiring people and I wanted to call you as soon as possible. You were a great employee and, as you know, we really didn't want to let you go! Will you come back to work for us?"

"Milstein, I really appreciate the offer. Can you please give me a few days to think it over?"

"Sure Kairo; give me a call when you've made a decision. Talk to you later." "Alright. Bye-bye, Milstein."

"Zealand! Zealand!" yelled Kairo in a loud, excited and urgent voice.

"Yes, honey."

"That was Milstein on the phone. Guess what? They want to give me my old job back!"

"It sounds to me like you're considering the offer?"

"Well, we really could use the money."

"Baby girl, we talked about this. You said you were somewhat relieved that you got laid off, right?"

"Well, I was because I could finally do what I always wanted to do—design clothes."

"So what changed your mind?" asked Zealand in a tone of exhaustion.

"I know that I have a talent for design. In fact, it's what I do best, and there're no designs out there quiet like mine, but…"

"But what?" asked Zealand.

After a long pause in the conversation, Kairo blurted, "Well, I'm scared! There, I said it! I'm scared! My old job provided security for us. Since the layoff, we've had to give up a lot of things, and you've had to work a lot of overtime."

"Hey, wait a minute. Don't use me as a scapegoat not to follow your dream!"

give your life 生 *away*

Our doubts are traitors and make us lose the good we oft might win by fearing to attempt.
~ Shakespeare

"Well, what if I fail? What if no one buys my designs? What if you lose your job and my design work isn't enough to meet our bills?" asked Kairo.

"What if this? What if that?" stated Zealand in an irritated tone. "The 'what if' I'm concerned about is, 'What if you go through the rest of your life regretting that you didn't take the opportunity to design clothes?' You made good money on your last job—and we sure enjoyed spending it—but you always complained that you weren't happy. Kairo, I 've never seen you more alive and happy, except the day you gazed upon my gorgeous face and Hercules-like body, than when you're in the den designing."

"You mean the day I saw you in your sister's yard wearing a greasy, stained white tee-shirt, worn, dirty jeans, sporting a beer belly, and a mullet?"

"Ha! Ha! Ha! The point is you really seem happy when you're designing. Now, you want to give that up out of fear of the 'what if's' and for so-called job security. You were laid off once; and it's a good chance you could get laid off again. There's no such thing as job security. Don't let your addiction to a job or fear of not having enough money, stop you from being a fashion designer."

Zealand continued, "I'll support you either way, but it seems to me that your fulfillment and happiness lies in doing what you do best. You must have the courage to cast the 'what if's' to the wind. Besides, I'm looking forward to the classic 1960 Jaguar that you're going to buy me with the money from your designs."

"Now I remember why I married you. You have a great since of humor," stated Kairo in a half-joking, half-sarcastic tone.

"Qué pasa (What's up) Salvador? Are you headed home for the holidays?" said Aalim.

"Yeah," Salvador stated with a dry tone.

"What's wrong? You should be excited about going home!"

give your life 生 *away*

When you fear something,
learn as much about it as you can.
Knowledge conquers fear.
~ Anonymous

69

"I am, but I'm not excited about telling my parents and grandparents that I want to leave college and become a clown. I'm terrified," stated Salvador.

"Are you still thinking about doing that clown thing?"

"Yeah man. I love making people laugh and I'm good at. I was supposed to be the first person in my family to complete college, get my MBA, and join the most prestigious investment firm in the country. You know the firm, the one that has all those commercials. I've been having this nightmare lately where I'm at home with my family when one of those commercials comes on television and the guy in the commercial puts his hands around a clown and says, 'We don't clown around with your money; we make it grow!' It would be a great commercial, but the clown happens to be me. Estoy sentado allí viendo el comercial con toda mi familia y están llorando porque les he hecho vergüenza."

"Hey wait a minute, Salvador. I don't speak Spanglish, dude! English please."

"I got a little excited. I'm sorry. What I said was that I am sitting there watching the commercial with my entire family and they're crying because I have caused them shame."

"Hey buddy! I would be terrified too. Why don't you finish college, and then become a clown?" stated Aalim.

"I thought about that, but I really can't stand being here doing something that I don't want to do. But if I don't stop being scared, I'll be here when I could be at Clown College learning to make people laugh under the big tent. If I fail as a clown, I'll just die. My family would most certainly disown me," stated Salvador in a particularly distraught fashion.

"Salvador, what I've discovered in my relatively short life is that the only person that you should be concerned about pleasing is yourself. You're the only person you'll ever really have the power to please. I know that your family has high hopes for you, but your life belongs to you and you must do with it what you believe is best. Trying to please others is not the way to happiness. Happiness is the way."

give your life 生 away

It is not because things are difficult that we do not dare,
It is because we do not dare that they are difficult.
~ Seneca

Salvador's look of surprise indicated to Aalim that Salvador had no idea Aalim could be so deep and profound.

Aalim continued, saying, "I've learned that most of our fears are imagined. You don't know for sure exactly how your family is going to react to your becoming a bozo. Hey, just kidding! You might be pleasantly surprised by their reaction. Look on the bright side, even if your worst fears are confirmed, your family will eventually get over your decision. Meanwhile, you'll be deliriously happy clowning around. And if they don't get over it, that's their problem. Don't let anyone's thoughts about you, or reactions to what you do in life, define who you are. Also, it's impossible to fail at doing something that you love. Remember, I've seen your clown routine and it's phenomenally funny, if 'phenomenally' is a word. That's the only way I can describe your gift. If this is of any consolation to you, I envy you. I don't know what I want to do with my life. I don't know what I'm really great at."

In a tone of astonishment at Aalim's words of wisdom, Salvador stated, "Thank you, thank you, thank you!"

"Just a few more miles to home," Salvador nervously thought to himself as he switched lanes on the expressway. As ironic and as corny as it might sound, the song "Send In The Clowns" played softly on his car radio. "Spooky", he thought to himself. Either he'd tell his family of his plans, or return to a life at college that he hates. Aalim's wise words had given him some relief and much-needed support. He thought now, with shame, that he shouldn't be afraid of how his family might react or that he might fail as a clown.

"This is insane. I must be some kind of idiot or fool to think about quitting my practice. I like being an ophthalmologist. It's great! The money is excellent, and I help all kinds of people, but I keep having thoughts that I had when I was younger. The thought of being a mechanic and having my own repair shop haunts me. In fact, this thought has nagged me most of my life, sometimes loud and clear and other

give your life 生 *away*

The courageous conquer fear by transcending it.
~ Anonymous

times a whisper. Just when I believe the thought is gone, it comes roaring back again. I was terrified to tell you; you might have me committed, or better yet, confined in a permanent medicated state," said Inga to her therapist in a half-joking, half-serious tone. "If it wasn't for the doctor-patient privilege, I wouldn't have shared this mechanic thing with you. Dr. Okoro. I can't get this nagging desire out of my head. I'm a great ophthalmologist, but I really excel when it comes to working on cars. I want to open an auto repair shop that caters to the needs of single moms, with reasonable rates, loaner cars, pick-up and drop-off service, babysitting on site, weekend and evening service, and female mechanics doing most of the work."

"Wow! You really have given this some major thought," responded Dr. Okoro in his African accent.

"So tell me, doctor, what should I do?" said Inga as she gazed out of a window in Dr. Okoro's nineteenth floor office overlooking sun-glazed Table Bay in Cape Town, South Africa.

"When did it become insane to do what you want to do in life? Besides, we have at least discovered during our time together that you're not insane…a little high strung and maybe a little paranoid, but not insane," stated Dr. Okoro.

"What ophthalmologist, especially at my age, would leave her practice to be a mechanic? I'll end up penniless and on the streets. It takes money to open an auto repair business. What will my family, friends, co-workers, and church members think?" stated Inga.

"So you're going to allow your age, thoughts of poverty, and what others think prevent you from doing with your life what you know you should do?"

"Well, I guess so. I don't know what to do, Dr. Okoro. The way I'm behaving is out of the ordinary for me. As you know, I've always been predictable, rational, and level-headed—that is, if we don't consider my high strung nature and that skosh of paranoia," stated Inga jokingly.

give your life 生 *away*

We create our experiences in life either you create fear or you don't – don't!
~ Ha-kim

"Listen to me, Inga, and listen well. I'm terribly serious right now! What you're considering may well be insane to others, but it's not what others think that matters. You have to muster the courage to overcome your fears, and do what that voice in your soul is telling you to do. If you live your life according to the way others want you to, you'll never be happy or fulfilled. That's because only you know what's best for you.

Family, friends, church members, co-workers and anyone else you can name rarely know what's best for themselves, not to mention what's best for someone else. And let me tell you something about that age thing: you're never too old to do what you think is best for yourself or what you have the talent to do. Remember, I didn't become a doctor until I was fifty-five. As long as there is breath in your body you're never too old, nor is it ever too late."

"As for this poverty thing, that won't happen to you. There might be some lean times in the beginning as you learn the auto repair business, but I know that you have the discipline to be frugal and to make good financial decisions. As your well-paid therapist, I've given you all the advice I can to help you overcome your fears. You must decide on your own if you have what it takes to conquer them. Our time is up. See you next week!"

Because using your unique talent to serve others is a drastic departure from the way that you've lived in the past, you'll probably have some fear of leaving the comfort of your current life. You'll probably experience the three greatest fears that most people have: the fear of failure, the fear of others' opinions, and the fear of poverty.

Kairo, Salvador, and Inga are not unlike most of us who allow the fear of failure, others' opinions, poverty, our age, our sex, our race, whether we are insane or crazy according to conventional wisdom, and our job addiction prevent us from doing what our soul cries out for us to do, what we know is our unique talent, what we love doing, what we

Most of our obstacles would melt away if,
instead of cowering
before them, we should make up our minds
to walk boldly through them.
~ Orison Swett Marden

know will bring us satisfaction, fulfillment, and prosperity.

The good news for Kairo, Salvador, Inga and you is that the antidote to any fear—without exception—is courage, the courage to eliminate your fears altogether or the courage to act despite your fears.

The best way to acquire the courage to eliminate fear altogether is to understand your fears and to put them in the proper perspective. Once you understand your fears and put them in the proper perspective, you'll realize that there's nothing to fear, or what you fear is only in your imagination and couldn't possibly occur, or what you fear might happen—but with some thought, planning, and action can be avoided.

Many great people will say that if they had to live life over again, they would fail more because they learned more from their failures than they did from their triumphs. Now, we all like to learn, and since failure is just another way of learning a lot of stuff, who's afraid of learning? I'm not; how about you?

An amazing inventor, Thomas Edison, described failure as a way of eliminating those things that don't work, which in turn bring you closer to that which does.

When it comes to understanding the fear of failure and putting it in the proper perspective, nearly every great person will also tell you that you can only fail if you give up. Once you decide that you're never going to give up, then you can't fail and there's no reason to fear something that can't happen.

Now, would you agree that understanding what failure is and putting it in the proper perspective really takes the boogeyman out of failing?

When it comes to understanding the fear of others' opinions and putting it in the proper perspective, most great people will tell you that what people think about you is none of your business. Some might even say it by using expletives. They say this because, as they journeyed down their path toward greatness, it was what they thought

give your life 生 *away*

I have lived a long life and had many troubles,
most of which never happened.
~ Mark Twain

about themselves that assured their greatness—not what others thought about them.

You give the opinions of others power when you agree with their opinions, decide that their opinions really matter in your life, or act according to their opinions. Believing that only the Creator and you know what's best for you takes the power away from what others think of you. Without power, the opinions of others are nothing to fear.

When it comes to understanding the fear of poverty and putting it in the proper perspective, you will realize that most of the people you see in our society that we consider impoverished—such as the homeless—are destitute because many of them (not all) suffer from a mental disease, a severe drug or alcohol addiction or an unforeseen catastrophic event for which they probably never received or wanted help.

It might be the case that you have friends or relatives who lost their homes and possessions after losing their jobs and found themselves destitute. They didn't have a mental disease or severe drug or alcoholic condition. Many people (but not everyone) who become destitute because of a job loss do so because they lived above their means, failed to seriously consider or plan for unexpected and unforeseen occurrences and the day that their livelihood or resources could or might end. If you fear that you might become destitute when you decide to give your life away in service to humanity by using your unique talent, start living below your means, and save the money necessary to cover your expenses as you transition into the life that you were intended to live.

You acquire the courage to act despite your fears by having confidence in your soul's voice, the same voice that revealed your unique talent. When you have confidence in your soul's voice that means that you trust that your divinity (Creator within) knows what's best for you. When you accept that your divinity knows what's best for you, you realize that you must do what your soul desires, no matter what.

give your life 生 *away*

Come to the edge, He said.
They Said, We are afraid.
Come to the edge, He said.
They came.
He pushed them, and they flew.
~ Guillaume Apollinaire

Knowing that you must do what your soul desires—no matter what—will give you the courage necessary to act, despite your fears.

give your life 生 *away*

You can not discover new oceans unless you have the
courage to lose sight of the shore.
~ Anonymous

Chapter 6

Why Is It Imperative That I Use My Unique Talent?

I expect to pass through this world but once,
and any good therefore that I can do,
or any kindness that I can show to my fellow creature,
let me do it now. Let me not defer or neglect it,
for I shall not pass this way again.
~ Stephen Grellet

He who has two coats,
let him share with him who has none;
and he who has food, let him do likewise.
~ John the Baptist

Some men see things the way they are and ask, "Why?"
I dream things that never were, and ask "Why not?"
~ George Bernard Shaw

"*RING*, ring, ring, ring. "You've reached the Fienbergs. We're not in" says Marina, "but if you leave your name," says Jay, "and the time you called," says Marina, "we'll call you back as soon as possible" Marina and Jay say in unison.

"Hey guys, this is Gilbert. I have bad news. Rickie Peters died last night. He was only 47 years old. He died of a heart attack. I thought you guys would like to know."

"Wow! That's sad," Vienna thought to herself as she listened to the numerous messages that had accumulated on the family answering machine during the day, while she was in school. "Beep," the answering machine went as she listened to the next message.

"Hey Vienna, this is Dae. There's a party at Morgan's house on Friday night. Do you want to go? I tried to leave a message on your mobile, but it sounded funny so I thought I'd leave one on your home phone." The remaining messages were for Vienna's brother Kori and from the usual telemarketing suspects.

Vienna thought she knew all of her parent's friends. The name Rickie Peters, however, didn't ring a bell. She never heard her parents talk about him. Usually she would leave the messages on the answering machine for her parents to retrieve, but because the message disturbed her she decided to deliver it to them personally. "Why at only 47, just one year younger than my parents, had Rickie Peters died of a heart attack? Don't only old people die of heart attacks? This might happen to mom and dad; they might die now since people around their age are dying," thought Vienna to herself.

Vienna was now determined to find out exactly who Rickie Peters was and why her parents hadn't mentioned him. Was he important to them? He must have been since Uncle Gilbert thought enough to call. She couldn't wait for her parents to get home from work.

Jay and Marina arrived home just as the sun descended beyond a parade of trees that stood in the distance in their wooded backyard. They found Vienna perched within a small alcove, just at the top of the stairs on the third level of their home. As her parents ascended the last step just before touching down on the third floor landing, Vienna uttered "Mom, Dad. I have some sad news. Rickie Peters died. Uncle Gilbert called, and said he died of a heart attack." Marina and Jay turned simultaneously and looked at each other with twin expressions of surprise and sadness. "Who was Rickie Peters?" stated Vienna.

"Give us a minute sweetheart, and I'll tell you about Rickie Peters," stated Jay.

After Jay and Marina were settled, Jay stated, "Rickie Peters and I went to college together. He actually married a childhood friend of mine, Natalia. Rickie was a funny, sweet soul but, unfortunately, he was the greatest animation artist that the world will never know. He was drawing animation by hand back in the seventies that animators are creating on computers today. This guy was at least 30 to 35 years ahead of his time. He always drew diverse racial and cultural male and female characters and gave them positive and heroic story lines. He actually called his characters the Rainbow Coloured People. The story lines focused on the characters living in peace and harmony having wonderful and adventurous escapades. He once spent hours telling me how he dreamed of bringing these characters to life on the big screen as human-like 3D animation and on the computer as 3D games that kids could play and learn from. The big screen, I thought, was a possibility—but the computer, that was an idea that was far out there at the time. Computers were very new and rare back then, but that was Rickie. He always saw things that the rest of us couldn't quiet envision. I have no doubt, especially when I compare the computer generated animation today with Rickie's hand-drawn animation, that he was the best in the world."

"Dad, did he ever do any of the things you guys talked about?"

give your life 生 *away*

No one respects a talent that is concealed.
~ Desiderius Erasmus

"He kept drawing for a few more years after we left college. The last time I talked to him, he informed me that he and Natalia had married. I learned several years later that they were the proud parents of eight children. I heard through the grapevine Rickie took dead end jobs that were convenient and routine to support his family. He probably got caught up in everydayness like all of us, and before he knew it, his dream became a blurry vision in the rearview mirror of his mind. Millions of kids who play computer games today would be exposed to games that value diversity, peace, learning, and fun as opposed to the violence and anger that's present in many of the video games today…if only Rickie would've just pursued his talent with a little passion. Vienna, please listen to me carefully! Are you listening?"

Vienna looked with bewilderment as her father spoke.

"I've learned that it's not as important to pursue your passion as it is to pursue your talent with passion." Several moments of silence hung in the air. "I'm sorry, sweetheart, I got a little emotional there; it's just that we all are less than what we could be when a talented person like Rickie loses sight of his dream and fails to pursue it."

"Mr. Peter's story makes me sad," stated Vienna.

"Let me call your uncle for details on Rickie's funeral. I'll also call Natalia and extend our condolences."

How is he today, Onawa?" stated Lakota as he walked into the hospital room of their father, Runningcloud.

"He has been drifting in and out of consciousness since I relieved you yesterday."

"Lakota, is that you?" said Runningcloud in a weak, barely audible voice.

"Yes! Dad, it's me. Don't try to talk; save your strength. Onawa, go home. You look awful! I'll stay with Dad."

"Lakota, call me at home after you speak to the doctor."

"Sure, just go before you collapse."

Onawa, with dark puffy circles under her eyes, the type that evolve when you hold vigil over a loved one in the hospital, leaned over her father's bed and gave him a kiss—the kind that said, "I love you, but this maybe the last time I see you alive." Onawa then proceeded home.

Runningcloud was 75 years old when the hospital claimed him as a resident after cancer invaded and began to conquer his body. Lakota pulled up a chair, nice and close to his father's hospital bed; if his father spoke, he didn't want him to strain to talk, nor did he want to miss the last word that might be uttered by a man that he loved more than life itself. As Lakota sat in the typical-looking hospital room, with all the fancy electrical equipment with wires leading from his dad to the equipment and all the usual equipment noises—bleep, bleep, bleep— he managed to dose off.

"Good morning" stated Runningcloud's doctor, in his French accent, which awakened Lakota from his two-minute nap.

"Good morning," stated Lakota in a startled voice.

"Sorry to wake you. I'm making my rounds, and I'm here to check on your father."

"I'm sorry I missed you yesterday, Dr. Jean-Paul. He's sleeping peacefully," stated Lakota.

"I don't think I need to wake him. Let me look at his chart; the nurse has already given me an update. Um huh, um huh," stated the doctor as he reviewed Runningcloud's chart.

"Doctor, my sister told me that he has been drifting in and out of consciousness."

"That's because of the medication," stated the doctor in a low voice. "We're making him as comfortable as possible under the circumstances. As I stated to you and your sister last week, he is in the terminal stage of his illness and his death may be imminent, but I hesitate saying that because no one knows for sure when the transition will occur. But until then, he'll be comfortable, pain-free, and treated with the utmost dignity. He may have periods when he'll be coherent and will speak to you as well as understand you. I don't need to tell you to cherish these coming moments. It's been a pleasure serving your father. He's so rich in wisdom. Is there anything that you need? I've ordered fresh sheets for your cot and a special meal will arrive from this great restaurant across the street. I asked your sister what was your favorite food. I know what it's like to care for a loved one in a hospital."

"Thanks! You didn't have to do that," stated Lakota with sincere gratitude.

"Yes, I did! That's what I do. The nurse, of course, will inform me if your father's condition changes. If so, I'll be here as soon as possible. See you later."

"Lakota! Lakota!" said Runningcloud in a weak voice.

"Yes, Dad."

"I'm so glad you're here, son. There are a few things I would like to tell you. I love you and I'm sorry."

"I love you too dad. What are you sorry for?"

"For not being a peacemaker."

"What do you mean, dad?"

"I think the term they use today is 'diplomat.' When I was in my early twenties, I actually attended college."

"I know that. You majored in something to do with agriculture, right?"

"Yes! But what you don't know is that while I attended college, there was a protest on campus by the students regarding financial investments the university had in companies in South Africa. The students wanted the university to divest itself of those investments in protest against the South African Government's policy of apartheid. Although I was not directly involved in the protest, I had friends that were. I shared a dorm room with one of them; he was my best friend. The students were having difficulties framing their demands and asked me to help. I made a few suggestions. They were so pleased with the suggestions that they chose me to present them to the administration. At first, I didn't want to get involved, but they convinced me that I could serve as a neutral party in the dispute. The administration agreed. The suggestions that I made to both parties prevented a takeover of the administration building by the students and a lock down of the university."

"Dad, don't you need to rest?"

"Lakota! I have to tell you this story; it explains why I'm sorry. As long as I can talk, let me. I was able to convince both parties to agree to a mutually beneficial course of action. I learned from that experience that I liked helping people and organizations resolve issues in a peaceful manner and that I was really good at it."

"Okay, Dad, that's great, but why are you sorry?"

"After this incident, I was chosen to serve on a board that resolved disputes between the administration and the students. I served on the board until I graduated. I was asked to speak at several colleges throughout the country, outlining my dispute resolution approaches. Just before graduation, I was approached by the administration and offered a scholarship to pursue a master's and a doctorate degree in International Affairs and Diplomacy, which was quite unusual for an indigenous person at that time. The hope was that I might someday serve in the United Nations as a diplomat, some type of peacekeeper or Ambassador. I knew, however, that I was needed at home on the farm and that... [Cough! Cough!]"

"Here Dad, drink this! Take it easy!"

"Okay, where was I?" stated Runningcloud as he recovered from his cough.

"You were telling me about being needed at home on the farm," stated Lakota in a cautious tone.

"When the Dean told mom and papa of their interest in providing me with further education, without hesitation they declined and said that as the oldest of my siblings, I was needed on our farm, and it was expected that I would take over the farm someday and continue to use it to support the future generations in our family."

"How did you feel about that?"

"I was distraught, but back in those days it was disrespectful to disobey your parents. I declined the scholarship and returned to the farm after graduation. Every day of my life, I've regretted my decision. I should've had the guts to follow my heart and use my talent to help people. I never told you or Onawa because I was ashamed and I didn't want the two of you to think that I was a coward."

"We would never think that!" stated Lakota.

"Our lives would've been different. Me, you, your sister, and your mother—rest her soul—would've traveled the world. Our lives would not have been such a struggle."

"We did alright, Dad. Me and Onawa got college degrees and great jobs."

"Son, doing alright is not good enough when you're placed on earth to be great. I could've helped the world by being in the United Nations; I could've taught countries how to exist in the world together in peace. I don't mean to sound arrogant or conceited, but most of the diplomats and world leaders today really don't know how to achieve or maintain peace between nations when disputes arise as evident by all the armed conflicts that exist between countries today. All I needed to do was get my mind around a problem and I could solve it peacefully. Because of my fear of disobeying my parents and my lack of courage, we live in a world without peace."

"Dad, that's not true. That's ridiculous; you're exaggerating. You aren't responsible for the unrest in the world."

"Yes! I'm partially responsible. We all are when we have the ability to do something about a problem, but instead, because of fear or comfort, we choose not to. You see, son, if we don't use our talent to solve a problem that only our particular talent can solve, no one else will because no one else has the same exact talent that we have. It's every person's obligation to solve the problem that their talent was given to them to solve; otherwise, the world's problems will never be resolved."

"Please understand how imperative it is that you and Onawa use your talents to better the condition of mankind right now; don't you and your sister wait another day. Don't wait until you get old, sick, and exhausted with regret before you understand and realize how important it is that you use your talent to help others. I've wanted to tell you this for a long time. I'm sorry I waited all these years. As much as I wish I could go back and change the past I can't. So please promise me that you and Onawa won't die with regret like me."

The long conversation took its toll on Runningcloud. His eye lids started to droop and his breathing became shallow. It seemed that he had saved up just the right measure of strength to confess his lifelong sorrow. He then fell into a deep sleep, but this time, strangely enough, Lakota noticed a peace that hadn't caught his attention when he earlier gazed upon his father as he slept.

Lakota couldn't help but replay every word his father had spoken during their prodigious conversation. For the first time in his life, he realized that he had a profound responsibility to use his talent to help people. He also appreciated that the failure to share his particular gift with the world could in all reality, as silly as it might have sounded an hour or so earlier, have an immense affect upon the course of human history.

After about an hour, Runningcloud awoke and directed Lakota to call Onawa and tell her to return to the hospital as soon as possible. He then drifted back to sleep. Lakota, fearing the inevitable, crawled into bed next to his dad and wrapped his arms gently around him. The doctor was summoned by the nurse at Lakota's request.

When Dr. Jean-Paul arrived, Lakota attempted to get up.

"Stay there. It's okay," said the doctor.

The results of Runningcloud's vital signs indicated that his transition from his current state of being to his next state of existence was imminent. Dr. Jean-Paul compassionately

*Whatever we possess becomes of double value when we
have the opportunity of sharing it with others.*
~ Jean-Nicolas Bouilly

held Runningcloud's hand, and in silence he seemed to bid him farewell and Godspeed on his next journey. He then told Lakota that he would be praying for him and Onawa. Softly, and in silence, he exited the room. Onawa then entered and sat on the left side of her dad. She didn't speak. The atmosphere in the room said it all.

Surprisingly, Runningcloud awoke from his slumber to find Onawa to his left and Lakota lying next to him and clenching him tightly around his shoulders.

"I love you, Onawa. I love you Lakota, but I'm tired. I want to go now to my ancestors," stated Runningcloud in a weak and barely audible voice.

"We love you, too," stated Onawa and Lakota with deep sadness.

Runningcloud then slipped into the sweet sleep of transition. For he was now on that white horse headed for the northern territory to be reunited with his ancestors, in the land of eternal peace.

"Click, hum------hum---click, hum----hum, click, click! Cluck!" went the garage door.

"Dad's home, Mom. He just drove into the garage!" stated Kai.

"Hello everyone," yelled Dr. Jean-Paul as he entered the spacious first level of his huge four-level home. He could hear a barely audible reply from three of his ten children. As he ascended to the third level he was greeted by Kai, Jade, and Ashley, "Hi Dad!" to which Dr. Jean-Paul replied, "Hello, beautiful girls." Each of Dr. Jean-Paul's three daughters kissed him, one by one. They were terribly glad to see him. It had been nearly 39 hours since he left home for the hospital. It was early evening and several of the children were involved in after school activities, and the rest were away at college.

"Where's my bride!"

"Mom's up in the attic," said Ashley.

"You better get up there dad. She's rounding things up

for charity again. You remember what happened the last time," stated Jade while trying to conceal her laughter.

"Yeah! I remember. She threw away my favorite soccer jersey that I wore as a kid growing up."

"Hi gorgeous!"

"Hello handsome!" could be heard by the girls as Dr. Jean-Paul and his bride of 30 years, Lola, exchanged romantic greetings as they had done almost every day since they met.

"I understand from the girls that you're collecting for charity. Is that my seminary year book?"

"Yes!"

"I haven't seen that in years."

"I found it hidden here in the floor board. I somehow must have overlooked it the last time I decided to clean out the attic," stated Lola with suspicion. "Handsome did you hide that from me?"

"Yes, honey I did. Girls! Oh Girls!" yelled Dr. Jean-Paul. The girls could be heard scurrying up the stairs to the attic!

"What's up dad?" said Jade.

"I want to share something with you! Look at this picture."

"Dad, why are you wearing that priest outfit?" stated Kai with a surprised look on her face.

"When were you a priest, dad?" said Ashley.

"You never told us you were a priest," said Jade.

"Mom, did you know that dad was a priest?" said Kai.

"Yes! Your father had just left the seminary and entered medical school when I met him."

Then came the most logical question. "Why did you leave the priesthood, dad?" all three girls asked in unison, which evoked laughter among everyone in attendance in the attic.

As the laughter flowed into silence, Dr. Jean-Paul stated, "I want to tell you a story. As a child, I was told by my parents, grandparents, and other relatives that the priesthood was the most admired calling that a person could have."

"Not Uncle Michel. He was a free spirit; he wouldn't have encouraged you to do that, dad?" stated Jade inquisitively.

"No, everyone but wonderful old Uncle Michel, may his soul rest in peace. Despite the family's concerted effort to push me toward the priesthood, I always had an interest in the medical field that addressed the health issues of those with terminal illnesses, especially cancer. I was always a very caring loving person, which pleased my mother; she just knew I would make an excellent priest. So I did what most people do—I capitulated to the whims and desires of those who thought they knew what was best for me. I went into the priesthood, although I wasn't sure it was right for me. I realized after much prayer, contemplation, and meditation while studying at the seminary that the purpose of my life was to be of service to others. I wasn't so sure I was cut out serving as a priest. I realized that the priesthood was a wonderful calling but that it wasn't calling me. I was wise enough to know that because I had a talent, interest, and a love for medicine that practicing medicine was the way the Creator intended that I should carry out my service to humanity. Girls that was the easy part."

Ring! Ring! Ring!

"Let it ring. What I have to say is very important."

"It's just Nikhil, based on the caller ID, calling for Jade. He likes her, dad!"

"Shut up, Ashley!" stated Jade in a tone of embarrassment that suggested that her parents may have just discovered the identity of her first male caller.

"We'll talk about Nikhil later, young lady!" says Lola in a stern and serious voice.

"Where was I?"

"Dad, you were about to tell us what happened when you decided to leave the seminary," stated Kai.

"Yes, right! The easy part about leaving the priesthood was knowing that I wanted to practice medicine, but the hard part was telling my parents and grandparents. I realized that to escape the wrath of my parents and grandparents, I had to have a terribly good reason for not being a priest. I therefore decided that when I spoke to my family I would speak from my soul. After all, it was my soul that had directed me to leave the priesthood and pursue medicine." "At a family meeting convened by yours truly, I started out with a nervous and trembling voice saying, 'I'm glad ah---- ah---- ah------- everyone could be here this evening. After much prayer, contemplation, and medication I mean meditation, I believe—no I'm sorry, I know—that the calling of my life and the lives of all people is to serve others."

"Well of course, son. That's why we encouraged you to become a priest," said my father in a very authoritative tone.

"With caution, I asked my dad and everyone else in the room to please not speak until I finished what I had to say. Everyone agreed. I went on to state that although everyone had the same calling in life, everyone fulfilled that calling differently based upon their talent. I explained that although I was a good priest, because I was given a greater love and talent for medicine, it was in that area that the Creator had decided that I was needed the most in carrying out my service. I then stated in a very hurried and soft voice that I would be leaving the priesthood and would pursue my life's calling—medicine."

"I told my family that I was confident that there were others who were given a talent for the priesthood and they could better serve others as priests than I could. Although I witnessed several changing facial expressions while speaking to my family—ranging from disapproval, to confusion, horror, to exhaustion—I made it a point to finish my statements. Most of my family was speechless, but knew me well enough to know that I always thought my decisions through carefully. They realized that it took a great deal of courage for me to decide to leave the priesthood, and to share the decision with them. Oh, there were the naysayers,

give your life 生 *away*

*If we have no peace, it is because we have forgotten
that we belong to each other.*
~ Mother Teresa

but as time went on, everyone realized that I made the right decision. They saw how happy, excited, and content I was practicing medicine."

"I remember my parents stating, some years after recuperating from my decision to leave the priesthood, that they were happy that I chose medicine. Girls, as I've told you, your brothers, and sisters over and over again, it's your calling in life to serve humanity."

"Yeah, yeah, Dad! We know we're supposed to use our unique talent to carry out that service," stated the girls in unison and in a tone that indicated they had talked about this nine hundred and ninety one times before and didn't want to talk about it again.

"Oh, Dad. Do we really have to hear that calling speech again? We understand, Dad. For the one millionth and one time, we know how imperative it is that we live according to the calling stuff. The Creator is counting on us to fulfill the needs of others in the world, needs that only we can fill by using our unique talent. We get it dad," stated the girls in chorus.

"Hey, Dad, what if I discover that my unique talent is dancing, and I run off to Latin America with a real cute hunk to learn the Tango? What do you think about that?" said Ashley with sarcasm.

"If you're sure that dancing is your unique talent and you'll serve others by dancing, then I'm all for it. But the hunk better be your husband."

"Hey, Dad, we love to joke with you about the calling stuff, but we know its importance. We want to be just as happy and content as you are and to create a life for our families like the one you and mom have made for us—not to mention all the money we have," stated Ashley.

"Correction—all the money your mom and I have! You and your brothers and sisters are broke! Honey before I forget, Mr. Runningcloud died last night!"

"I'm terribly sorry to hear that sweetheart; you told me

that he was a wonderful man."

"Yes he was. It was a pleasure to be able to care for such a great man during such a difficult and sad time. He shared his rich heritage with me and I'm grateful. But you know honey, as long as I've been a doctor, I still marvel at how much joy I get from treating my patients. This talk took longer than I wanted it too."

"Dad, you know how you are when you get on a roll," stated Kai.

"I'm tried; I think I'll take a long nap. Hey, honey, if Nikhil calls for Jade, or if Ashley's hunk calls, tell them to call back in let's say 30 years!"

There are unique needs that humanity has that only you can fulfill by serving and carrying out that service through the use of your unique talent. No one else can or will meet those unique needs because no one else has the same unique talent that you have. Remember there is one thing you do, in the way that you do, better than anyone else in the world, and if you don't use that talent, those in need of it won't receive the help they need and desire. Your unique talent may be cancer research. You may be the very person who will discover the cure for this monster, but if you don't use your talent, people will continue to suffer and die from this merciless killer when they don't have to.

If your unique talent is raising and caring for children, it's imperative that you devote your life to parenting. The world hungers for children who become men and women of character, love, compassion, nobility, integrity, strength, wisdom, peace, and kindness—those who are independent and march to the beat of the unique rhythm in their souls. If your unique talent is philanthropy or feeding the hungry, it's imperative that you use that talent to help those who toll in the ugly dark abyss of poverty and hunger who live and die without ever experiencing dignified shelter or a satisfied stomach. Therefore, because others are depending on you, it's imperative that you serve and carry out that service by using your unique talent.

Don't underestimate the power of your service and how you, as one individual, can influence the world. Yes, you! Expressing your unique talent in service to others is powerful enough to set in motion a miraculous change in the world. If Rickie Peters would've had the courage to pursue his talent for animation with passion, it's possible that we would live in a society where everyone embraces and values cultural and racial differences. If Runningcloud would've used his talent for peacemaking we couldn't help but wonder whether the word war would still exist in our world vocabulary.

The description of the effects of Rickie Peters and Runningcloud's unique talents on the world might appear to be extreme or unrealistic to you (is your ego back), but the power of service through the expression of our unique talents has no limitations. Just remember the effects of your neighbor, Gandhi, your mother, Jesus of Nazareth, your father, Martin Luther King, Jr., your grandfather, Mother Teresa, your grandmother, Muhammad, your sister, Harriet Tubman, your brother, Thomas Edison, Steve Jobs, your aunt, Buddha, your uncle, Aung San Suu Kyi, your cousin, Wright brothers, yourself, Bill Gates, and Nelson Mandela, among many.

Dr. Jean-Paul is the poster person for those who use their unique talent to serve. He discovered why he is here, the calling of his life. He discovered his unique talent for practicing medicine in a silent place, and he had the courage despite his family's wishes to pursue the use of that talent in service to humanity. He fulfills the needs of his patients with his unique talent by skillfully and lovingly helping them transition from this life to the next existence in a most dignified and comfortable manner. The unintended reward of his service is permanent fulfillment, lasting happiness, prosperity, and, of course, material wealth.

Not only is it imperative that you use your unique talent in service to others, but it's essential to your life if you yearn to experience permanent satisfaction and fulfillment, lasting joy and happiness, and prosperity.

I must admit that my motives for writing this chapter are selfish because I imagine living in a world where no need goes unfulfilled. I imagine a world where there is no more fear, fear-mongering, violence, war, war-mongering, hunger, racism, sexism, hatred, poverty, destruction—but rather, acceptance, love, peace, harmony, happiness, compassion, joy, creation, abundance, and prosperity.

I imagine a world in which those with the unique talent for peacemaking will eliminate war and warmongering and establish peace. I imagine a world in which those with the unique talent for showing, expressing, and giving love will eliminate fear, hate, and anger and establish love and compassion. I imagine a world in which those with the unique talent for creating harmony would eliminate chaos and establish calm and order. I imagine a world in which those with a unique talent for creating wealth will forever eliminate poverty and establish infinite prosperity and abundance. I imagine a world where those with the unique talent for elevating and lifting others will eliminate low to no self-esteem and self-worth and establish towering human significance and soaring human greatness. On and on it goes until all of humankind's needs are met.

If you're saying to yourself that such a world is not possible, that means your ego has returned and is putting up unnecessary illogical resistance to this provocative idea. So long EGO! When we give our lives away in service to others by using our unique talent, we are in connection with the Creator and all that the Creator is—love, joy, beauty, peace, kindness, and abundance.

You're the most magnificent, exalted, and miraculous, creation and as such—according to Jesus of Nazareth—you have the power to work even greater miracles than him, who, among many things healed the sick, fed the hungry, and loved the loveless. So, I beseech thee to be courageous and give you life away in service to humanity through the use of your unique talent, and watch for the magnificent things that will happen in your life and in the lives of those you serve. You will be astonished!

Be ashamed to die until you have won some victory for humanity.
~ Horace Mann

Chapter 7

How Do I Stay On Calling My Entire Life?

You get what you strive for.
~ Qu'ran

*If you would hit the mark, you must aim
a little above it, every arrow that flies feels
the attraction of earth.*
~ Longfellow

*This one thing I do,
forgetting those things which are behind,
and reaching forth unto those things which are before,
I press toward the mark!*
~ Bible

give your life 生 away

"VOCÊ diz que você está mochila através de Portugal. Por que?" (You say you're backpacking through Portugal. Why?) stated the Merchant. "Acabei de grad school na Espanha e precisam de tempo apenas para limpar a minha cabeça e decidir o que eu quero fazer com o resto da minha vida." (I just finished grad school in Spain and need time just to clear my head, and decide what I want to do with the rest of my life) stated Vãn as he reached for a banana while handing the merchant money. "Boa sorte e ser seguro." (Good luck and be safe) stated the merchant as Vãn proceeded through the open market.

"Teaching languages to kids in Southeast Asia and Africa would be cool, but mom wants me to join her architecture firm; the money would be sweet, though. Arctic weather research with Yotimo would be a blast. Maybe I'll join my buddy Salvador at Clown College." Vãn's eclectic thoughts of the future took him into a thousand mental directions as he walked in the crisp air of Lisbon in search of a hostel.

"Rain, great Christmas party," stated Ms. Chen, Rain's boss, chairperson and founder of the company "8Red Wire Global."

"Yes it is!" responded Rain.

Ms. Chen, handing Rain an envelope, continued. "You've been doing a great job for the company, but the board of directors and I have decided to take the company in a new direction. Regrettably, that means we will have to let you go. You'll find that your severance package is very generous." For several weeks these stunning words echoed in the hollow passages of Rain's mind over and over and over.

Eventually the word hit the street that the hottest rising COO on the planet was inexplicably available. Rain was suddenly swamped with jobs offers. Despite these offers, she found herself unexpectedly and inexplicably perusing a list she'd managed to write while mourning her loss.

- Non-profit that makes micro business loans to indigenous people living on reservations. - Teach International Business

107

Etiquette to women - Open SPA for single mothers and their teenage daughters - (Note to self) - Get out of storage my demo tapes, songs, and musical arrangements that I wrote while in college.

"Uncle Indu, I was just promoted to director of human resources. I wanted you to be the first to know," stated Sandari with excitement.

After a long pause in the conversation, Uncle Indu stated, in a tone of doubt, "That's great news Sundari, isn't it?"

"Why of course it is. Why did you say isn't it? I really thought you would be happy for me," retorted Sundari.

"It's just that in light of our last conversation, when we talked about your desire to be a travel documentarian or sportswriter, I'm a little doubtful that this promotion is really the direction you want to go in."

"Oh! Uncle you can be quite negative sometimes," stated Sundari as she abruptly hung the phone up without allowing Uncle Indu to speak or telling him goodbye.

Uncle Indu wasn't just a relative; he was Sundari's best friend, her confidante, someone whose wisdom and advice she cherished and respected above all else.

"Hello," stated Uncle Indu as he answered his phone.

"Uncle I'm so sorry. I shouldn't have spoken to you that way; please, please, please, forgive me," stated Sundari while crying.

"Of course, my sweet child, I forgive you. Stop crying," stated Uncle Indu in a very lighthearted tone.

"It's just that because of this promotion, I've become confused about what direction I should take my life. I thought that if you where overly excited about the promotion, I would take that as a sign that I made the right decision. I was trying to take the easy way out," stated Sundari with a mixture of relief and shame.

"My dear child I've always told you to intelligently weigh your options and that I would never tell you which choice to make, and I won't start today."

"I have a lot to think about. Again, I'm so sorry for my disrespectful behavior," stated Sundari in a tone of regret and genuine sorrow.

"Shut up child. I'll be there for Thursday night dinner; I'm bringing the Kheer," stated Uncle Indu cheerfully.

"I love your Kheer. I almost forgot Liv, my chef friend from America is going to cook several surprise dishes. You're going to love her cooking; it's beyond this world. Bye Bye Uncle!" stated Sundari as she politely hung up the phone.

Once you've decided to live your life on calling (giving your life away in service to humanity), you'll want to stay on calling your entire life especially in light of the wonderful unintended benefits that you'll enjoy.

During your life, you will be faced with significant, life-changing decisions. You may be faced with those decisions early in life, like Văn; you may be forced to consider them when you least expect it, maybe after being fired like Rain; you may be faced with them when a great opportunity like a promotion comes along, as with Sundari.

The best way to insure that you stay on *calling* your entire life is to ask yourself the very important *calling question* before making any significant, life-changing decisions.

The *calling question* is: *Will this decision allow me to use my unique talent to help others (serve humanity) without the expectation of receiving anything in return, not even a thank-you?*

If you answer "Yes" to this question when making life-changing decisions, you will spend your entire life *on calling* and reap the unbelievable unintended gifts.

Example: Let's say that you're a high school or college student on the adulthood journey and you're contemplating becoming an architect. *As an architect, will I use my unique talent to help others (serve humanity) without the expectation of receiving anything in return, not even a thank-you?*

Planning, designing, and overseeing the construction of

buildings will help others by providing them with wonderful and spectacular spaces to enjoy. You love the thought of helping people as an architect so much that you would plan, design, and oversee the construction of buildings for free if you could afford to. If your unique talent is planning, designing, and overseeing the construction of buildings, then you would answer "Yes" to the calling question. Because you answered "Yes," you should seriously consider giving your life away in service to humanity as an architect.

Although planning, designing, and overseeing the construction of buildings are helpful acts, you won't be living your calling by being an architect if you don't have a unique talent for them. Maybe your unique talent is teaching and training young people how to run competitively. You might want to consider coaching middle or high school track. Coaching young people is a helpful, loving act. Sports help the young through the awkward period of juvenile maturation. You love the thought of coaching young people so much that you would coach them without the expectation of receiving anything in return, not even a thank-you. The unique needs of those for your unique talent will be met; no one else on the planet could coach track in the unique way that you would.

Example: Let's say that you're on the middle-age journey and, after several years in a particular profession, you're contemplating owning a spa. *As a spa owner, will I use my unique talent to help others (serve humanity) without the expectation of receiving anything in return, not even a thank-you?*

Providing a relaxed environment in which people can escape the everydayness of their lives and be pampered is a loving, helpful act. You love the thought of helping people as a spa owner so much that you would provide a relaxed environment in which to pamper them for free if you could afford to. If your unique talent is the ability to provide relaxed and pampered accommodations for those seeking a temporary escape from their lives, then you would answer "Yes" to the calling question. Because you answered "Yes," you should seriously consider giving your life away in service to humanity as a spa owner.

Although owning a spa is a loving, helpful act, you won't be living your calling by owning a spa if you don't have a unique talent for it. Maybe your unique talent is providing a service which helps property owners decorate their living spaces. You might what to consider owning an interior design firm. Designing interiors that allow people to more fully enjoy their property is a helpful act. You love the thought of helping people by providing an interior design service so much that you would provide it for free if you could afford to. The unique needs of those for your unique talent will be met, no one else on the planet could provide interior design services in the unique way that you would.

Example: Let's say that you're on the mature-age journey and you're contemplating becoming a tour guide. *As a tour guide, will I use my unique talent to help others (serve humanity) without the expectation of receiving anything in return, not even a thank-you?*

Conducting tours of various destinations of interest and providing specialized knowledge on subjects such as art or architecture about those destinations is helpful to those who hope to increase their knowledge and enrich themselves. You love the thought of helping others as a tour guide so much that you would conduct tours and provide specialized knowledge about various destinations for free if you could afford to. If your unique talent is providing specialized knowledge about various travel destinations and sharing that information with tourist, while conducting tours, you would answer "Yes" to the calling question. Because you answered "Yes," you should seriously consider giving your life away in service to humanity as a tour guide.

Although providing specialized knowledge about various travel destinations while conducting tours is a helpful act, you won't be living your calling by being a tour guide if you don't have a unique talent for it. Maybe your unique talent is raising money for charitable organizations. You might want to consider starting a philanthropic organization. Raising money for worthy projects that would otherwise not be funded is a loving, helpful act. You love the thought of philanthropy that you would raise money for worthy projects without the expectation of receiving anything in return, not even a thank-you. The unique need of those for your unique talent will be met; no one else on the planet could raise money in the unique way that you would.

You, along with Vãn, Rain, and Sundari, might be tempted from time to time to ignore the calling question when making significant, life-changing decisions, to instead consider what is popular, hot, or politically correct, what might bring recognition and power, what others think, or how much money is involved. However, if you consider the *calling question* before making significant, life-changing decisions, there is a good chance that you'll give your life away in service and thereby be on calling your entire life and enjoy the permanent, miraculous, fulfilling, and unintended benefits derived from doing so.

To ease your mind, understand that non-life-changing, everyday decisions to serve humanity—such as lending a helping hand to someone, returning a smile, sending a silent prayer, or the commission of an intentional random act of kindness—don't have to be decided by asking yourself the *calling question*. When making these decisions, let the kindness in your heart and the divine wisdom in your soul lead you to serve in a way that is most helpful at the time.

I'm feeling a little melancholy now because our majestic journey together is quickly coming to a close.

give your life 生 *away*

*All who have accomplished great things
have had a great aim,
have fixed their gaze on a goal which was high,
one which sometimes seemed impossible.*
~ Orison Swett Marden

Chapter 8

Dance To The Unique Rhythm In My Soul?

If a person does not keep pace with their companions,
perhaps it is because they hear a different drummer.
Let them step to the music which they hear,
however measured or far away.
~ Henry David Thoreau

Let the immortal depth of your soul lead you.
~ Anonymous

We ought to dance with rapture
that we might be alive...and part of the living, incarnate
cosmos.
~ D.H. Lawrence

WHEN it comes to living, understanding, and accepting the calling of life, servants hear a different rhythmic beat than most people; they hear the unique rhythm in their souls. Servants must dance (live) according to that unique rhythm (Divine Guidance). Their divinity and genius lies in dancing to that rhythm. Servants understand that everyone has a unique rhythm in their soul, just as great musicians have their very own distinctive sound and unique expression.

Servants know that to dance to the unique rhythm in their souls means to give their lives away in service to humanity through the use of their unique talent, a talent which allows them to do a certain thing in the way that they do it, better than anyone else on the planet and better than anyone in history. The splendid unintentional gifts of the dance are permanent fulfillment and satisfaction, lasting happiness, peace, and prosperity. Servants therefore accept that this life is not about them, or they would have been created to toil in isolation doing things to please themselves and no one else. (Is your ego upset?)

When servants dance, they may seem detached from society's idea of what the purpose of life is—such as so-called success, career, money, recognition, or power. To some, the detachment is viewed as hubris, arrogance, or aloofness. Servants, however, aren't distracted by these views; they go on dancing with the confidence that service to humanity is the true calling of life.

Servants dance in the present, the here, and now. They're too busy calmly serving in the moment to concern themselves with what happened in the past and what will or will not happen in the future.

Servants are focused on dancing to the unique rhythm of their soul, while others are distracted by irrelevant banter, fear-mongering, what naysayers are pontificating, or the latest juicy celebrity gossip. Such distractions go unnoticed by servants as they dance with undiminished focus.

Servants don't dance according to the unique rhythms

found in the souls of others (parents, friends, relatives, pop culture, or society), nor do they dance according to what others think or how others want them to live their lives. Servants know that by choosing to dance to someone else's rhythm, their dance will be awkward (make poor choices, live a life not their own) and off beat (stressful, without purpose, or direction) as opposed to balanced, steady, and beautiful (living the life the Creator intended for them and reaping the fabulous gifts). Servants know that it's an insult to their very soul to dance to someone else's rhythm because in doing so they neglect the dance the Creator wisely intended for them.

Servants are wise not to allow the rhythm found in society's tune of conformity—that encourages everyone to act, look, think, and behave the same—distract them from their dance. They know that most people are distracted by the rhythm of conformity to the neglect of their own unique rhythm, because they want be liked and to fit in, please others, please their egos, or they fear dancing to the unique rhythm of their own soul.

When servants hear the rhythm found in society's tunes of profession, business, career, occupation, or job, they respond by dancing to the more noble unique rhythm in their soul, *life's calling*. Servants dance to the rhythm of life's calling by giving their lives away in service to others (humanity) without the expectation of receiving anything in return, not even a thank-you.

The servant's dance to the rhythm of life's calling illustrates the servant's understanding that serving humanity and carrying out that service by using their unique talent is far more significant, meaningful, and imperative than simply having a career, earning a paycheck, or achieving so-called success.

Once servants have discovered their unique talent (maybe it's choreography), they don't think of choreography as simply a profession, career, business, or job; they view choreography as a divine mission—their life's calling. The

And those who were seen dancing were thought to be insane by those who could not hear the music.
~ Nietzsche

servant will throw their whole heart and soul into choreography. Through choreography, the servant will seek to improve the condition of humankind. The servant will give their lives away in service to humanity as a choreographer without the expectation of receiving anything in return, not even a thank-you.

Dancing to the rhythm of life's calling allows the servant to experience unintended permanent spiritual gifts, (joy, prosperity, fulfillment, and greatness) which they know are far superior than the societal rewards (money, power, success, or recognition) offered by the societal tunes profession, business, career, occupation, or job.

Therefore, servants are never motivated or influenced by societal rewards when making decisions. Societal reward is not the focus. The servant's focus and motivation in the dance is always service, not the rewards of service. However, servants wisely know that when they dance to the rhythm of life's calling, they will enjoy both permanent spiritual gifts and societal rewards.

Servants respond to the rhythm of the world, as it relates to the needs of humanity, by dancing in such a way that their service reaches and touches as many lives as possible. Servants realize that the lives that their dance is intended to serve depend on their dance. They understand that because their dance is unique to them, that if they don't dance, then the needs of those for their unique dance will go unmet or unfulfilled.

Servants never take their responsibility to dance to the unique rhythm of their souls for granted; they intentionally seek out opportunities everyday of their lives to serve others. For example, saying "Hello" to those in the waiting room of a doctor's office or hospital or those standing in a elevator, smiling at someone with sincerity, asking someone how they are and really caring, saying a silent prayer for a passing hearse, fire truck, police car, or ambulance, laughing with a child, telling an elderly person how much they're valued, or

give your life 生 *away*

Movements are as eloquent as words.
~ Isadora Duncan

telling others that they love them. Random acts of kindness aren't random for servants. They're a daily part of a servant's life.

Servants have discovered that there are actually more opportunities to serve than their ability to met those opportunities and therefore understand why it's vital that everyone chooses to serve. Servants realize that if everyone gave their lives away in service, every need on the globe for peace, love, compassion, harmony, and racial, ethnic, religious, and cultural empathy would be met.

Servants respond to the rhythm of the world, as it relates to physical health, by dancing to the rhythm that the body is the sanctuary which houses their divinity and, as such, has miraculous powers to heal itself—as long as they are gentle with it and give it the care it needs. Such care includes eating healthy foods, eating in moderation, routine and effective exercise, getting sufficient rest, and nonuse of such toxins as cigarettes, cigars, and harmful drugs.

Servants realize that it's extremely important to be physically fit, not just for their own well-being but also for the benefit of those that they serve. They understand that being unhealthy will diminish their capacity to dance and meet the needs of those that depend on them. In addition, servants understand that they must consistently involve themselves in activities that will assure good mental health. Such activities include daily meditation, communing with nature, and a life-long practice of banishing external and internal noise when they feel they've lost their mental balance. Other activities include striving to maintain and improve mental acuity through activities that are challenging, inspiring, and refreshing to the mind and soul, communing with those who have high positive energy, and learning to respond automatically to any situation with towering constructive emotional control as opposed to low-lying, uncontrolled, negative emotions, and attitudes. Excellent mental and physical health allows servants to effortlessly dance while

give your life 生 *away*

*Let the day be lost to us on which
we did not dance once.*
~ Nietzsche

meeting the needs of others.

Servants respond to the rhythm of society as it relates to the elderly by dancing to the rhythm that the elderly are the possessors of valuable secrets and great wisdom and, therefore, should be highly respected. Servants embrace the notion that a great deal can be learned by spending as little as a few minutes with the elderly. They possess the wisdom of the ages and can share the secret and what courage is necessary to take kindly the counsel of the years and to gracefully leave behind the things of youth.

Servants respond to the rhythm of the world as it relates to children by dancing to the rhythm in their soul that the choice to have and raise children is of a noble and high calling. Therefore, children shouldn't be born into the world or adopted to satisfy selfish desires, but because they are needed in a world of unrest, intolerance, and indifference to be ambassadors of peace, love, happiness, compassion, and of course service.

Servants dance to the rhythm of raising children by teaching them as early as possible the calling of life. Servants in their dance have the courage to allow children with minimal guidance (guidance that will keep a child from danger and harm) to discover their unique talent, while mindful of the miraculous, fulfilling, joyful, and prosperous life that awaits a child who gives their life away in service to others.

Servants back off on occasion to allow the child in its dance to embrace its divinity. They don't interrupt the child's dance with such old tunes as, "No, don't do that," "Do it because I said so," "I think you should do this or that with your life," "Life would be easier if you would just try to fit in," and "Get a good education, so you can get a good job." Instead, they introduce the child to such rare tunes as, "Follow your soul's voice," "You're worthy of everything," "You don't discover your life you create it," "Giving your life away in service will allow you to experience your highest magnificent self (love)," and "Your genius lies in being, not doing."

Servants respond to the rhythm of the world as it relates to their material possessions by dancing to the unique rhythm in their souls that any possessions that they have aren't owned by them, but loaned to them by the Creator to be enjoyed and used in their service to humanity. They are humbled and eternally grateful for the unlimited possessions that show up in their lives and the opportunity to enjoy and use those possessions in service. They are confident that as long as they serve, all they need will show up in their lives.

Because servants have no attachment or ownership claim to the material possessions that show up in their lives, they never boast or brag about possessions and, therefore, don't dance to the rhythm that their self-worth and value is measured by what possessions they enjoy. Servants understand that low self-esteem, disappointment, despair, unrest, fear, and unhappiness occur when the ego is allowed to define their self-worth. The servant's motto of self worth, as articulated in the introduction is: *I am a divine expression and extension of the Creator. Therefore, I am complete and there is nothing I can do or acquire that will make me more perfect and precious than I am at this very moment.*

Servants respond to the rhythm of the world as it relates to the earth, nature, and the universe by dancing to the rhythm that everything and everyone is connected. When they view nature, the universe, and the earth, they see the Creator and themselves in every person, every animal, the oceans, the seas, rivers, mountains, hills, valleys, planets, the stars, the moon, and the sun.

Servants in their dance are eternally awed, humbled, and grateful for the dance of the universe, the earth, and nature. Servants' awe and gratitude are shown in their dance when they protect the universe, earth, and nature from acts by humanity that are harmful or destructive.

Servants respond to the rhythm of the world as it relates

to the Creator (whatever they perceive the Creator to be) by dancing to the unique rhythm in their soul that they're the ultimate expression of the Creator's divinity and, therefore, their souls are that part of the Creator's spirit that went into making them. Because they possess a part of the Creator's spirit, they dance as divine infinite spirits, not as temporary humans with ego-driven lives, intentions, motives and actions. They know that because they possess a part of the Creator's spirit, they have the power to manifest or create anything they desire without worry, unreasonable sacrifice or dogged determination, but with love, calm, ease, and patience. You can determine from their movements during their dance that they're confident and that they think from the end.

They visualize themselves first in possession of what they desire to create in their lives to assist them in their dance, they stay focused on that desire and, before long, it appears. Servants know from experience that there's never a reason to worry or fall into despair when something they desire doesn't appear immediately. The servant is not attached to how, when, or in what form the assistance shows up. In their divine wisdom, they know that what they desire is on its way and will appear exactly on time and are grateful when it does.

You can determine from servants' movements during their dance that they, unlike most people, are truly happy, and fulfilled. They don't want for things; they are the things that they want. They don't want peace; they are peace. They don't want love; they are love—a love that they freely give away. They don't want to care; they are caring. They don't want abundance; they are abundance. They don't want harmony; they are harmony. They don't want to be happy or joyous; they are happy and joyous.

Although servants may or may not be associated with any particular religious group, they in their dance respect all such groups with the knowledge that everyone and everything is

give your life 生 *away*

Dancing is the loftiest, the most moving,
the most beautiful of the arts, because it is no mere
translation or abstraction from life: it is life itself.
~ Havelock Ellis

connected with the same calling, to serve humanity.

Servants dance according to the unique rhythm of their soul in such a way that when watching them, you get the feeling that they're convinced that all of humanity's problems could be solved if every person chose to give their lives away in service.

Just a short glimpse of servants dancing conveys that the performance of their service—through the use of their unique talent—is natural and effortless. They appear to be floating on a cloud without any concern with the confidence that they're performing their dance as the Creator intended.

Those who observe the dance of servants are amazed by how content, serene, and prosperous they are although they live in a world where there is war, war-mongering, hate, fear, fear-mongering, chaos, disease, suffering, crime, poverty, and an epidemic of low to no self-esteem, integrity, self-love, self-trust or self-respect. Servants happily dance under such circumstances because, in the depth of their souls, they know that their dance will help improve the condition of humankind.

Servants joyously dance on, no matter what turn the economy takes, what political party is in control of the government, whether it was a good or bad day on Wall Street, or how much death and destruction is reported in the media; they know that humanity needs their dance.

So, I say to you my precious friend, dance the servant's dance according to the unique rhythm of your soul—for the entire world to see. The world hungers and thirsts for your dance. It needs your dance; it is depending on your dance, it's imperative. All of humanity, your family, friends, and loved ones need to see you dance. No one who has *lived*, is *living* or will *live* can dance your unique dance; therefore if you don't dance to the unique rhythm of your soul, all of humanity will be at a loss. Try to imagine what would've happened if Gandhi, Martin Luther King, Jr., Muhammad, Buddha, Jesus of Nazareth, Mother Teresa, Harriet Tubman,

Thomas Edison, Steve Jobs, Bill Gates, Aung San Suu Kyi, and Nelson Mandela, just to name a few, had not danced to the unique rhythm in their souls and given their lives away in service to us.

I beseech thee to dance! If you only knew how wonderful and beautiful your life would be if you danced the servant's dance. I can see you now how effortless your movements, how sweet your steps. There's no greater beauty than seeing you dance to the unique rhythm of your soul! Again, there is nothing on earth that you can do that would bring you staggering joy, majestic peace, and prodigious love than giving you life away in service to others. So go now and dance, dance the servant's dance!

I extend to you greatness and all the unimaginable gifts of a life devoted to serving humanity. See you at the dance!

I love you!
Your Servant,
~ çì-ỳàì

But when you do dance, I wish you o' the sea,
that you might ever do nothing but that.
~ Shakespeare

give your life 生 away

P.S. You thought that this volume had ended. Just a few last words as we conclude our magical journey together.

I want you to know that success is no longer good enough for you,

for success is the achievement of a goal any goal. A common criminal can be successful. You must be great, for greatness is the achievement of a goal whose chief aim is to serve humanity.

~ Ha-kim

Will you, won't you, will you, won't you,
will you join the dance?
~ Lewis Carroll

The End
La fin
Konec
Slut
Край
Het einde
Lõpp
Loppu
ةياهنلا
Das Ende
Τέλος
li fini
חוסה
Vége
Akhir
La fine
beigas
pabaiga
slutten
Koniec
Fim
Sfârşit
Конец
konec
Fin
Slutet
Son
Кінець
Kết thúc

about the author

Very little is known about this mysterious author.

This is the very little that is known:

The author knows that the only purpose for human existence is to be of service to one another. The author desires from the marrow in the author's soul that each individual give their life away in service to others to improve the condition of humanity.

The author's only impetus for writing is to convince humankind that each individual has a unique talent that all of humanity would benefit from if that individual would just give their life away in service to others through the use of that talent and that each individual would experience immense joy from doing so.